Every once in a while you read a book that touches your soul, engages your heart, and pushes your mind to look at the world in a new way. Jessica Bryan's flowing and absorbing narrative invites the reader to live her journey and return transformed.

—Vicky Thompson
New Connexion Magazine

Jessica has captured the spirit of the Filipino people and the Philippine Islands. Her intimate bonding with the characters and the detailed account of her interactions with the culture will help readers understand Filipino psychology and the principles of psychic surgery.

—Virgil J. Mayor Apostol
Rumsua: Ancestral Traditions

This refreshingly honest and well-crafted book makes for enjoyable, inspiring, and informative reading. In addition to telling a remarkable story, the book explores psychic surgery and faith healing in depth. After turning the last page, I came away wondering when the sequel will be released.

—Andrea Kremko, D.D.
The Ashland Oracle

This book details the author's fascinating experiences in the Philippines and has plenty of humor. I enjoyed reading about my Filipino culture as seen through the eyes of someone from another county.

—Godofredo "Butch" Stuart, M.D.

This exploration of the intriguing and mysterious world of psychic surgery and faith healing is engaging and informative. The writing is open-hearted, appealing, and refreshingly direct.

—Margie McArthur, author of *Faery Healing: The Lore and the Legacy*

Psychic Surgery

and

Faith Healing

An Exploration of Multi-Dimensional Realities,
Indigenous Healing, and Medical Miracles
in the Philippine Lowlands

JESSICA BRYAN

San Francisco, CA / Newburyport, MA

This edition first published in 2008 by
Red Wheel/Weiser, LLC
With offices at:
500 Third Street, Suite 230
San Francisco, CA 94107
www.redwheelweiser.com

ISBN: 978-1-57863-441-5
Library of Congress Cataloging-in-Publication Data is available upon request.

Cover design by Kathryn Sky-Peck
Text design by Cristy Collins, Creations Design
Typeset in Palatino
Cover illustration © Franz von Stuck
Author photograph: Joan Emm

Printed in the United States of America
TS
10 9 8 7 6 5 4 3 2 1

⊕ Text paper contains a minimum of 30% post-consumer-waste material.

Dedicated to
Rev. Filomena "Mely" Naces
and
Rev. Connie L. Arismende

*The light of the body is the eye: if therefore thine eye be single,
thy whole body shall be full of light.*
St. Matthew 6:22

*The primary mission of spiritual healing is not the elimination
of physical ailments, but to promote inner awareness, a sense of
spiritual attachment, and a personal fellowship with God.*
Rev. Alex Orbito

God only takes away what you are willing to let go of.
Rev. Connie Arismende

Acknowledgments

My gratitude and blessings to:

Tom Clunie, D.C., my loving partner, who supported me throughout the process of writing this book and offered many helpful suggestions.

The courageous and talented women of the Coquille Writers Group: Jane Morgan, Vesta Brownell, and Jessie, for their ongoing attention to detail and keeping me on track.

June McCourtney, for her generous spirit and enthusiasm.

Violet Young and Sinclair Lingg of the Holistic Health, Psychic, and Crafts Fair in Yachats, Oregon; Kate McDaniel; ATP®; Angel Therapist™; and Andrea Kremko of the Psychic and Holistic Faire in Grants Pass, Oregon for giving me the opportunity to learn more about mediumship and healing.

Godofredo "Butch" Stuart for adding details about Filipino culture and for posting excerpts from this book on his Web site at *www.stuartxchange.org.*

Virgil J. Mayor Apostol, who corrected my Filipino spelling and urged me to include "more romance."

Jerry Thompson and Reverend Ramon.

And finally, a very special thank you to Damiana L. Eugenio, Professor Emeritus, and the University of the Philippines Press for allowing the use of the Filipino proverbs originally collected in *Philippine Folk Literature: The Proverbs,* and to the other authors and publishers who have allowed me to quote from their work.

Contents

Preface

Ang hindi lumingon sa pinanggalingan ay di makararating sa paroroonan.
He who does not look back whence he came will not reach his destination.

PSYCHIC SURGERY & FAITH HEALING is a true story about my experiences with the psychic surgeons in Pangasinan Province, located on the Island of Luzon in the Philippines—including my initiation as a *magnetic healer.* The book also contains an essay entitled *The Miracle and the Enigma of Psychic Surgery.* This essay explores the metaphysical phenomenon of psychic surgery, and includes definitions, history, and quotes from other sources. The book is based on four trips I made to the Philippines between 1990 and 1994, but to avoid confusion, I have combined these four trips into two.

The Miracle and the Enigma begins on page 9 and appears interspersed throughout the book in separate callout sections, to be read as a continuously-running chapter contained within the more lyrical narrative. It can be read first in its entirety; the story can be read first; or they can be read simultaneously. Hopefully, readers will find this format entertaining as well as informative.

This book offers an in-depth look at the interplay between the world of physical reality and the world of Spirit. Although research into quantum physics is getting closer and closer to a scientific explanation for phenomena such as psychic surgery, and more and more people are talking about *energy medicine,* it is likely this thought-provoking book will raise as many questions as it answers.

After a brief introduction, the story begins at the Faith in God Spiritual Church, near Reno, Nevada, where I experienced psychic surgery for the first time with Rev. Connie Arismende and met Rev.

Filomena "Mely" Naces, who invited me to visit her in Pangasinan Province. Parts 2 and 3 take place in the Philippines. Section 4, *The Reluctant Healer,* explores magnetic healing, including some of the more interesting healings I have facilitated.

Section 5, *Simple Energy Healing Techniques,* contains instructions about how to use energy and meditation to help heal yourself and others.

Each chapter begins with a Filipino proverb that relates to the theme of the chapter. Also included are references for *The Miracle and the Enigma,* additional reading suggestions, travel resources, how to find a healer, and a list of Bible verses where healing is discussed. The real names of the healers have been used, but the names of the other people in this book have been changed to protect their privacy.

I was affected by my experiences with the psychic surgeons in ways I never expected, and for which I will be forever grateful. The process of writing this memoir has helped me understand what happened when I met these incredible healers—and then became a healer myself.

Jessica Bryan
Talent, Oregon, 2008

Far Out in Reno

The Aberrant Cell

Ang guinapangita mo karon, kalipay mo buas.
What you seek now is your happiness tomorrow.

I was born with a thorn in my side: one tiny, aberrant cell, different from all the others. Even as I lay curled small within the womb of my mother, my thumb in my not-quite-yet mouth, the imperfection created itself in silence, unnoticed, certainly by me. But as I grew older, and not necessarily any smarter or more aware, my obsession with perfection would collide in a major way with this infinitesimal bit of flesh.

I was born a girl, and this in itself can be difficult. Perhaps my soul incarnated in the twentieth century not quite ready to be female, unprepared for the tempestuous roaring of the tides, the obedience to the whims of the moon. Perhaps some Higher Power felt I was ready for the greater challenge of being female, after having lived many past lives as a man. Then again, maybe it was my higher self—like they talk about in Vedanta—that decided, "Yep, female this time." But these things are laid down, layer upon layer, cell upon cell, lifetime after lifetime, and I guess it comes down to trying to understand the complexities of karma, the intricate meaning of cause and effect.

Whatever the reason, the aberrant cell was there within the wall of my womb, given to me by my mother. I carried it with me through all the tumultuous years of my youth, a small burden, unnoticed until the age of thirty-nine, when I found myself at the doctor's office, legs spread, feet in the stirrups, listening to the doctor announce casually, "You have a fibroid tumor."

Did I eat too much ice cream, or not enough? Did I have too many heartless lovers? Was my own anger feeding the lump at the bottom of my belly? Perhaps it was the summer I was ten, when my father lost his job for the umpteenth time and I was forced to eat nothing but canned raviolis and shredded coconut for months. Maybe all that gummy pasta contributed to my imperfection—or was it his rage and my mother's fear of him that set me blundering through the world, careening and crashing, only to end up on that table listening to something I could not accept.

⋯⋯✳⋯⋯

Aberrant: to go astray; deviating from the usual or natural; atypical.
Research has shown that women who develop a nonmalignant
fibroid tumor of the uterus might have been
born with the cell from which the tumor originated.

After thirty-nine years of trying to be perfect, I had failed. A defect in my carefully contrived façade had been detected. I raged against it. I drank lime-flavored hydrogen peroxide to kill it. I spent thousands of dollars on vitamin pills and the pain medication prescribed by the doctor until they gave me an ulcer. I went to Chinatown for a potion, a lotion. I had a dream: an older man with a serious look on his face, dressed in a navy blue suit and carrying a briefcase, greets me. He looks into my eyes with compassion and says, "You have an *eleoma* and it's not spreading." Then gently taking my hand into his, he puts two capsules in my palm. Pointing to them, he says, "Take these, chaparral and red clover."

The next day at the library, I discovered my dream-doctor's meaning in a medical dictionary: "Eleoma: a tumor or swelling caused by the injection of oil into the tissues." There it was—the evidence of my sin—the French fries and cream donuts of my youth. Chaparral and red clover? These are traditional American Indian remedies for any type of tumor.

Later, after several years of attacking the aberrant cell, which by then had become ten centimeters of joined cells, and each month enduring the pain many women endure (only more so), I realized it would never leave willingly. It had been there since that undifferentiated beginning and my body did not recognize it as foreign.

I grew more desperate. I went to workshops in Santa Barbara, where I drew pictures with red crayons of the unwanted thing inside of me. I "dialogued" with it, urging it to dissolve. Ultimately, I decided to stop attacking my body and be kinder to myself. I began to meditate, visualizing the tumor dissolving in love and light.

Weary and running out of options—and just short of modern medicine's unacceptable answer for everything, the knife—I got in my car and drove to the Faith in God Spiritual Church in Lemmon Valley, Nevada to consult Connie Arismende, a psychic surgeon and faith healer. It was midsummer, 1990.

Surrender

Say kapalaran aga nibatikan.
No man can avoid his fate.

Beneath the baggy, ankle-length, white polyester gown closed with pink Velcro at the neck I am completely naked, and although the room is quite chilly, my hands and feet are sweating. I begin to shiver, and wonder if it is from the cold or because I am frightened.

The feeling of peace pervading the room seems somehow unbelievable, and I question whether the others waiting silently in the chairs around me are really as serene as they appear to be, or whether they are inwardly as nervous as I am. It is a moment of incredible inner struggle. I am held captive by desire and morbid curiosity. After coming so far and with such great expectations, I cannot just get up and leave.

An older man is touched lightly on the shoulder by a tall woman, who is also wearing a white robe. He rises at her touch and enters a door on one side of the room. After a few minutes, the door opens again so he can exit and another person can enter. One by one, they go in and out. As each person exits, they are led to a chair in the center of the room, where the hostess waves her hands softly in the air around them. When she is finished, she leans over and whispers something in each person's ear. Perhaps she is saying, "God bless you."

I look for obvious signs of emotion or trauma, but for the most part my fellow seekers seem only slightly dazed. Some have red eyes as if from crying, and I can smell the familiar odor of Tiger Balm as they pass by the chair where I await my turn. Some appear to be talking to themselves; maybe they are praying. I am grateful for the soft music coming in over the speakers because I am worried there might be sounds coming from the other side of the door that I would rather not hear. I feel as if some part of me is about to be sacrificed, or is it a baptism I have chosen?

My feet are ensconced in pink booties, and they rest on the thick, white carpet. Somehow the white of the carpet seems wrong. *There will be blood, won't there, even with this kind of miraculous surgery? How do they keep the blood from staining the carpet?*

The walls of the anteroom are painted sky blue and covered with embossed paper pictures of angels glued at random angles. They float amid fluffy clouds that have been painted on with a sponge. There are seven chairs arranged in a semicircle facing one wall, in the center of which is a life-sized stained glass portrait of Jesus. The gaze of his blue eyes is penetrating. His raised hands face outward as if he is blessing everyone in the room. Two stained glass doves hang from the ceiling in front of him. Pink candles, incense, flowers, and an open Bible with worn pages and obvious underlinings lie at his feet on a slightly raised platform. We are, it seems, also called here for worship.

When my turn comes, I pass through the door. The first thing I notice in the simply furnished healing room is a toilet in full view. *How could anyone use a toilet in full view?* There is also a vinyl-covered massage table, a hook on the wall to hang your clothes on, a counter holding a rice-cooker for heating massage oil, and a large pile of paper towels.

The psychic surgeon, Connie Arismende, stands at the end of the table, bracing herself against it as if to force her body to remain upright. Her expression is one of concern, concentration, and impatience. She seems totally focused and uninterested in idle conversation, nor is she interested in medical case histories.

Her assistant Coco, who is also her husband, instructs me to take off my gown, leave on the booties, and lie face down on the table. As he presses several paper towels along the sides of my body, I experience an even stronger inner conflict. The familiar feels safe, even if it is a painful illness. Lying on Connie's table for the first time is a major leap into unknown territory.

◦◦◁▣✳▣▷◦◦

People who undergo psychic surgery usually do not feel any pain because the energy field of the healer creates a condition known as *psychic anesthesia*. As Connie moves towards me at the side of the table, my awareness is thrust into the very center of my head—that boundless bit of consciousness containing the entire universe and everything I know as my *self*. It is a place of tranquil stillness, where I can hardly feel my body at all. I float weightless, filled with joy and a rainbow of colors.

Yet, seemingly far away as if happening to someone else, I hear noisy, slapping, wet sounds and smell the pungent odor of my own blood as it runs down my sides. I feel Connie's fingers pulling at something deep within me, first down the edges of my spine, then the backs of my knees and, after asking me to turn over, deep into my stomach. As I return dreamily to normal awareness, Coco begins to enthusiastically wipe away the blood with paper towels. Then he massages my body with warm mentholated oil. Throughout the experience, I am unable, or unwilling, to open my eyes to see what has been removed.

Afterwards, I sit in a chair in the anteroom and the hostess waves her hands in the air around me, as she did with the others. Stunned and unsure of what just happened, I float in a place far from normal consciousness. I am a paper angel on a blue wall, surrounded by clouds.

The Miracle
and the Enigma
of Psychic Surgery

In the Philippines, psychic surgery is sometimes referred to as *faith healing*, because faith in God is usually required. The terms *psychic surgery*, *faith healing*, and *spiritual healing* are used interchangeably throughout this book.

This phenomenon is usually viewed from one of two diametrically opposed viewpoints:

◆ It is a miraculous gift from God that produces physical, mental, emotional, and spiritual healing.

◆ It is a fake show using animal parts, water that has been dyed red, and cotton balls. The "healers" who take the public's money for a bloody performance are considered mere charlatans. (1)

Psychic surgery can also be explained in other ways, one of which is the placebo effect, meaning that people recover from a wide variety of illnesses after visiting a psychic surgeon because they believe they are going to be healed.

Continued on page 14.

The Faith in God Spiritual Church
in Lemmon Valley

◦◦⬤⬤✳⬤◦◦

Capayawat mo ava, as didiuen mo u ries.
Do not just swim, but feel the direction of the current.

The Faith In God Spiritual Church in Lemmon Valley, just outside of Reno, Nevada, no longer exists. But from 1986 until sometime around the year 2000, it was filled with spiritual seekers. Most of them suffered from some malady of body or soul, but some went only because they were curious. After leaving the surreal colors and flashing lights of Reno behind and driving north about ten miles on Highway 395 toward Susanville, the Lemmon Valley exit was easy to find.

The Arismende property was located at the end of a dusty road that wound its way through a long valley surrounded by haze-covered mountains. The peacefulness of the landscape stood in strange juxtaposition to the sordid chaos of Reno. The church was housed in a small chapel adjacent to Connie and Coco's double-wide mobile home. There was an outdoor patio with a vine-covered trellis that served as a roof. A lush, green lawn surrounded the house and church, but stopped abruptly at the point where the sprinkler system ended, leaving barren desert beyond to the south. This stark contrast made the church property seem like an isolated oasis both from Reno and the surrounding desert. To the north, there was a ranch with several donkeys. They were in a corral adjacent to the church lawn, and they seemed bored as they gazed at us through the fence.

◦◦⬤⬤✳⬤◦◦

Promptly at 10:00 A.M. on Sunday mornings, Connie would burst out of the door of the double-wide mobile in her bare feet, often wearing an ankle-length, white, Mexican dress embroidered with brightly-colored flowers. We would form a line and follow her into the church after paying $20 at the door, the charge for healing. Each person would sign a release form and write their name on a list, which would be used later to determine the order in which healing was received.

The release form was also posted prominently on the wall. It emphasized that only God can heal and Connie is merely an instrument of the Lord. It included this statement: *DO NOT STOP SEEING YOUR MEDICAL DOCTOR UNTIL YOU ARE RELEASED FROM TREATMENT. TAKE YOUR PRESCRIBED MEDICATIONS UNTIL THE DOCTOR GIVES YOU PERMISSION TO STOP.* By signing the release form, each person promised they would not hold Connie or the church liable if they were unhappy with their experience.

The sanctuary was filled with light, and birds could be heard singing through the open windows. It held about forty chairs. In the center of the room was a concrete pillar that had been painted lavender and covered with purple ribbons, each bearing the name of someone who had been baptized by Connie.

There was a large altar at the front of the room holding a portrait of Jesus, flowers (both plastic and real), bottles of massage oil, and photographs of people in need of *absent* healing—meaning they were not physically present, but would be given spiritual blessings from a distance. The congregants also put jewelry, bottles of water, and eyeglasses on the altar so these objects and the relationships they represent can be blessed at the appropriate moment in the service.

One wall of the sanctuary and the hallway leading to the bathrooms and changing areas were covered with paintings done by Connie. They represented visions she had seen in dreams and meditation. Most of them depicted the same thing: a spaceship that was going to bring Jesus back to Earth for the Second Coming at some future, undetermined date. Connie claimed it was written in one of the Lost Books of the Bible that He would return to Earth in an airship fifty miles long and fifty miles wide. It would be so big that it would blot out the light of the sun for three days. These paintings were curiously detailed and colorful, even though Connie was not a trained artist. The interior of the ship was laid out as a geometrical grid, with each section about half an inch square. It was as if she had actually seen the ship and rendered it photographically with a paintbrush.

"We made a total of nineteen trips to the Philippines. The healers saved my husband's life."

I smiled at the composed, older woman sitting across the picnic table from me in the church courtyard, encouraging her to continue. She relaxed in her chair, a slight breeze ruffling her graying hair, the sun shining gently on her face.

"He was diagnosed in 1988 with advanced cancer of the bladder and metastases throughout his body. They gave him six months to live, or less. In desperation, we booked a trip to Manila to see Alex Orbito, the Filipino psychic surgeon."

"How did you manage, with him so sick and all?"

"By the time we arrived in Honolulu to change planes, Joe had not urinated for three days, and I had to make a difficult decision. I knew if I put him in the hospital to drain his bladder they might keep him and he would never get out alive. On the other hand, if we continued on to Manila, he might die en route. We prayed to the Lord and continued on."

"Was the surgery successful?"

She nodded "Yes" and raised her hand, pointing to a handsome and rather dignified-looking gentleman standing across the courtyard. "See, there is my husband, Joe. He is over seventy now, and has been free of cancer for a long time. Reverend Orbito removed nineteen tumors from his body and they never grew back. We are here so Connie can check his heart." She continued to gaze at her husband as if she was surprised he was still alive.

I carefully considered my own situation. The miracle I sought had not yet manifested, even though I had been making the long drive from Berkeley almost every Sunday for months. I did not understand why others around me experienced dramatic results but I did not. I wondered why some people are healed instantly, some later, and some never. There are those who find spiritual, mental, and emotional peace through psychic surgery and faith healing, yet still succumb to physical disease and death. There are also skeptics with no faith whatsoever, who visit a healer, intent on exposing fraud, but instead recover their health.

Perhaps we choose our own destiny, time and time again. Some people believe each soul lives multiple lifetimes in order to learn specific lessons, and that we choose our parents and other circumstances. Even our manner of death is predetermined. Essentially, we create our own personal "classroom" on Earth.

I wanted to take personal responsibility for my thoughts and actions, because I know the body cannot be healed if the mind embraces sickness. I wanted to uncover my deeply buried feelings of guilt, grief, and anger, and release them. I struggled with my limited understanding. I was still looking for someone or something outside of myself to step in and save me, when what I really needed was to ask God for help and then *recognize* that help when it arrived. Healing requires faith, but it also requires receptivity and a willingness to be more closely connected to spirit.

When I told my doctor I was going to a faith healer for psychic surgery, she said she did not understand what it was but to keep doing it. Fibroids in women my age usually grow quite large, whereas mine had not grown at all. So I pressed on. I was like someone who develops an irresistible hunger for delicious food after tasting it for the first time. I craved the spiritual nourishment I received at the Church in Lemmon Valley, and soon it no longer mattered so much whether I had a tumor or not. I became focused on the greater healing, central to which was my goal of overcoming negativity and self-doubt.

The Miracle and the Enigma

Another possible explanation is that trickery is intentionally employed by the healers because they know an observable experience is needed in order for healing to occur. In other words, the healers create a dramatic show using fake blood and other props so people will believe in the most important aspect of healing, which is spiritual.

Some people believe the body is actually opened and the hands of the healer enter the patient's body. This is sometimes referred to as *bare-handed surgery*. The healer's hands function like *magnets* inside the body, drawing diseased tissue toward them, which is then removed and thrown away.

Simply put, the body is opened in much the same way as medical doctors do when using a scalpel, except that in psychic surgery there is no cutting, no anesthesia is used, and there is no pain, scars, or infection. The incisions can even be made by the healer merely pointing a finger at the skin of the patient from a distance of up to one foot away.

Continued on page 19.

Connie Arismende: Psychic Surgeon

Ti ulidan iturongna tayo, iti nalinteg a dalan.
A good leader will take us on the right path.

She smokes cigarettes. She eats baloney. She serves us Kool-Aid and hot dogs. Yet we, Connie's health-conscious devotees from California—who normally fill our plates with organic vegetables and vitamin pills—we seekers after purity eye the greasy potato salad and chips made with hydrogenated oil, and we are filled with confusion. She is our leader, our compass, the center around which we circle. Tethered to her by a fine, invisible thread woven of faith and our need to make sense of the world and our individual suffering, we sit in the courtyard after the Sunday service eyeing lunch wearily and struggling to understand what is required of us in order to attain inner peace and physical health.

Connie grabs me in her firm mental grip and shakes me until my narrow-minded ignorance begins to evaporate. She sets me squarely in her sights and demands that I confront my limitations, my sense of worthlessness, and the negativity instilled in me by my mother. She requires only that I become something bigger, grander, more in the image of God. She tells the congregation weekly that He only takes away what we are willing to let go of. She must be right, because after my first visit to Lemmon Valley I cried for two weeks, lost twelve pounds, left a destructive relationship, and, most importantly, resolved to never let anyone mistreat me again, NO MATTER WHAT.

Around the time she was painting her series of spaceships, Connie announced she was a *walk-in* from *Pleiades*. The Pleiades star cluster, also known as the *Seven Sisters*, holds a prominent place in ancient mythology. Only a handful of its many stars are visible to the naked eye.

A *walk-in* is a spirit that takes over a human body, usually when a person suffers clinical death and is then revived. It is similar to having a multiple personality. The original human identity remains deeply buried in the psyche, while the discarnate soul (or *walk-in*) inhabits the body and animates it. How Connie came to the conclusion she is a walk-in from Pleiades is a mystery, but perhaps it is the result of seeing a UFO in the Nevada desert when she was thirteen years old. When she preaches passionately about this experience and her Pleiades connection, as she often does, her skin seems to grow greener, deeper in hue. Her eyes become big, black, and bottomless.

Connie is a study in contradictions. She is as big an enigma as the healing she does on Sunday. One moment she seems transcendental, floating several inches above the ground. The next, she can be observed harshly criticizing someone while chain-smoking. She appears to be filled with jealousy and material desires, but she is also an amazing healer and teacher. *She must lie awake at night wondering who or what she is and examining God's purpose for her life.*

We celebrated the anniversary of the founding of the church every year on Memorial Day Weekend. My first experience of this special event was in 1991, the second year I was going to Lemmon Valley. There were services followed by healing each morning, and a firewalk was held outside in the driveway on Saturday night. This is a ceremony during which people walk barefoot on embers or hot stones. Connie said it was the culmination of the entire year, a time when we could attain great spiritual understanding.

I took my friend Sara with me that weekend. We had been friends for many years, after meeting at a yoga and meditation center in Texas. We had helped each other through divorce and sickness, and quite by chance we moved to California at the same time. Sara was originally from England. She did not have a physical illness, but she was curious about psychic surgery and welcomed the experience with an open heart. We drove to Nevada, attended the first service of the three-day weekend, and then after lunch . . .

I am lying on a table in Connie's healing room, but this time there are two tables crowded into the small space. Sara is lying on the table next to me. Romy Bugarin, a Filipino healer who is visiting from Texas, is about to perform psychic surgery on her.

Connie begins to dig her fingers deep into the area of my liver. I am unable to watch, even though I want to, because if I raise my head while lying on my back my stomach muscles tighten and this works against what she is doing. Connie moves quickly up my body, and soon she is pressing firmly into my eyes. There is some pain, but it only lasts for a moment.

As she continues to press, I feel something in the center of my head start to move slowly, but deliberately, towards her hand. I open my eyes just in time to see a stringy piece of white tissue about two inches long emerge from my left eye. Connie holds it up in front of me for a few seconds so we can both get a good look at it. Then she tosses it in the plastic bucket at her feet. Finally, she wipes my face with damp paper towels to wash away the blood and applies a small amount of mentholated oil.

Connie said later the tissue was from my pineal gland.

My experience is so intense that I do not look over at Sara until she is putting on her gown, her session with Romy complete. Returning to the changing area, which is crowded with other women in various states of undress, I examine the skin on my stomach. There are a few bright, red marks, but I know they will fade away within a few hours.

I look in the mirror at my eyes. At first, they seem normal, only a bit red as if they have been rubbed. Then I realize the quality of my vision is somehow different. My ability to "see" has changed. Things are brighter, more focused, as if a veil has been lifted. I make a note to visit the optometrist when I return to Berkeley to see if my vision has improved.

In fact, for the first time in thirty years, the doctor lowered the strength of my prescription.

Sara has not said a word since we left the healing room. She seems stunned, her face blanched white, her English sensibilities in turmoil. We leave the church and lie on the grass in the backyard.

The grass looks greener than any grass I have ever seen—as if I am seeing the color green for the first time. Although I have never taken psychedelic drugs, I imagine this must be what it feels like. Something happens and you feel alive for the first time; everything in your life before that moment was only a dream in preparation for this *coming alive*. The entire universe pulses within you. Your heart has become the heart of the universe.

Sara whispers something, but her voice is so soft I cannot hear what she is saying. Then louder, "JESSIE, SHE PUT HER HAND INSIDE YOUR STOMACH. YOU WERE BLEEDING. SHE REMOVED SOMETHING FROM YOUR EYE. I SAW HER DO IT."

We stare at each other for a few moments, speechless and unable to comprehend what has just happened. Sara has seen what I could not, what I dare not see: the reality of psychic surgery.

The Miracle
and the Enigma

Another theory holds that the psychic surgeons use an extrasensory skill called *psychokinesis,* which is the ability to move objects from one place to another using the power of the mind. As applied to psychic surgery, tumors, other bodily tissues, blood, and even foreign objects are dematerialized from within the body and then rematerialized in the hands of the healers on the surface. Psychokinesis is discussed in depth by the German physicist Dr. Alfred Stelter in his book *PSI Healing.* (2) This phenomenon has confused scientists for years, especially when the tissue samples removed by psychic surgery mysteriously disappear from the laboratory. (3)

Is it possible that chronic and incurable diseases can be treated successfully by mere faith? Do the Filipino healers have the power to open up a human body using only their bare hands, remove tumors or other diseased tissue in just a few minutes, and then close up incisions, leaving no trace? Many of the people who have been healed of serious illness by psychic surgery believe this is true. They believe they have been granted a personal miracle.

Continued on page 23.

The Firewalk

◦◦═✳═◦◦

Naglikay sa siga nasaugba so baga.
Trying to evade the fire, he plunged into the embers.

A photograph of Connie and Filomena "Mely" Naces—the Founder of the Faith in God Spiritual Church in the Philippines—hung on the wall of the chapel. It showed them walking across a bed of fiery coals. In the photos, they are holding hands and their arms are raised as if they are reaching to heaven while they make the short, ecstatic dance across the fire.

Firewalking is a technique for turning fear into power, and also a ritual cleansing. God tests us with fire to increase our faith. This is a deep lesson: As we conquer our fear of the physical fire, we come to terms with the fire of our passions and dreams. We break out of our limited view of ourselves and accept our physical mortality and spiritual immortality.

I attended the firewalk in Lemmon Valley three times. About forty people usually attended, not all of them "walkers." On Saturday afternoon, there would be a flurry of activity and phone calls to the local fire chief, who would wait until the last possible moment before granting the permit for an open fire. I imagined him outside in back of the firehouse, one hand on a cordless phone and the other held high in the air, testing the wind, waiting for a sign indicating it was safe to let those crazy people at the end of the valley have their fire. I never knew if he was aware of the reason for the permit. Maybe he thought we were roasting marshmallows and hotdogs.

While the fire chief weighed the weather, Coco considered the wood. He held each piece thoughtfully for a few moments before gently laying it on the pile in the driveway. Short, with legs like small tree trunks, he would occasionally pause and run his calloused hands through his thick black hair as he scanned the summer sky looking for his own sign.

Coco was a quiet, contemplative man, and I never heard him say much, except once. I was on the healing table trying to avoid Connie's attempts to penetrate my overly-sensitive throat when he said, "Jessica. You never gonna get married, 'cause how your husband gonna hold you down in bed when you wiggle so much."

Coco would receive the call from the fire chief around 6 P.M., and then immediately light the fire. While the rest of us were eating dinner in the courtyard, he would lean on his rake in the timeless manner of farmers everywhere and observe his handiwork. When the wood had burned down sufficiently, he would slowly rake out the glowing coals into a thin layer about six feet wide and ten feet long. We would have finished dinner by this time, the sky would be dark except for a few early stars and a brilliant full moon, and we would be in the church preparing to "walk the fire."

◦◦◁▱✳▱▷◦◦

"God is telling you it's safe to walk if your feet begin to tingle," says Connie.

We are sitting in a large circle listening to her preach on the meaning of the firewalk and how it relates to spirituality and healing. Her face is dreamy, her voice insistent. She appears to have shifted into a trance state.

"Follow the guidance of Jesus. Leave your burdens behind in the fire and allow yourself to be renewed. If He tells you to walk, then WALK."

One by one, people begin to stand up and drift outside. They stand in a line at the edge of the fire pit waiting for their turn. Others, including me, stand around the sides of the fire watching the glowing coals, the cold night air failing to penetrate us. If Jesus has commanded us to walk, we have not yet heard Him.

I attempt to reconcile a lifetime of teaching: "Don't touch that. You'll get burned," with what I see before me, as one by one and two by two they dance across, some shouting, "Praise God." This is not the Girl Scout camp of my youth. There are no campfire songs here, only the pounding of my heart as I stand on the damp grass.

◦◦◁▱✳▱▷◦◦

The firewalk I attended in 1991 was without incident, but many of the participants were burned in 1992.

"I built the fire with oak and it burned too hot," said Coco.

"They lost their faith," said Connie.

"The old man broke the spell" said several others.

The "old man" was a Filipino from San Jose, who refused to attend the prayer session before walking. He said he did not need to pray, but preferred to sit outside smoking cigarettes. When it was his turn to walk, he stopped in the middle of the open pit of coals for no apparent reason. He looked down, and perhaps realizing the enormity of where he was and what he was doing, he staggered and almost fell. Then he ran to the end of the fire pit and collapsed. His family carried him to the car. We later heard he was in the hospital.

The night the old man faltered, many of the other walkers lost their concentration and were burned. They sat up all night commiserating, with their feet in buckets of cold water. Even Connie was up most of the night with her feet in the toilet because there were not enough buckets. I lay in my tent under the desert sky listening to the snoring of the donkeys and pondering the reasons why some are burned and some are not, and why some (like me) are not brave enough or stupid enough to try to walk on fire. Perhaps it is just too much to expect that just as Jesus walked on water, humans can walk on fire.

The Miracle and the Enigma

In her book *Going Within: A Guide for Inner Transformation*, Shirley MacLaine describes her meeting with Alex Orbito, one of the most highly regarded Filipino healers, commenting, "Something we don't understand is occurring, and I believe it is evidence of alternative realities and higher-dimensional capability." (4)

MacLaine also relates an extraordinary experience with Orbito that involved placing her hand inside the open abdomen of a friend under his guidance. She describes the dissociative nature of her experience in this way, "It was as though my hand had a mind and spirit of its own, unconnected to my brain."

Many unusual psychic experiences and events cannot be explained, perhaps because we do not yet understand the scientific principles behind them. According to the physicist Dr. Andreas Freund, "Perhaps what we need to develop is a new science, a *metascience* [in order to understand this phenomenon]." (5)

Continued on page 35.

The Baptism and an Invitation

Ang kahilum sa tubig maoy timaan, sa kalalum ug katinawan.
The silence of the water indicates depth and clearness.

When someone asks my religion, I tell them whichever one they prefer. I have been almost all of them. After starting out as a Methodist at the age of five, I became a Presbyterian at eight because we had moved to a town where there were no other Methodists. Why I was sent to church remains a mystery, because neither of my parents ever went. I liked Sunday school, especially eating the white paste we used to glue little pictures of Jesus and Mary on our papers. It had a comforting wintergreen flavor.

At age nine, I met a man in the park near my house about an hour before dark. He approached me as I was looking for rose quartz to add to the collection I kept under my bed. We began to talk about God, and I told him to be careful when he stepped on the grass because the grass was God, too, and could also feel pain. I liked him because he seemed to understand the mysteries underlying the "real" world, and how children live fully in those mysteries.

My mother came looking for me. She seemed upset, and told me to go home while she stayed behind to talk to the man. Before I left, he gave me a small Bible and a silvery-blue, mirrored wall plaque depicting Mary cradling a sleepy Baby Jesus. It hung over my bed for years. Looking back, I question who the man was and what he was really looking for when he approached me in the park.

The next day, my mother told me the man had said I would be a saint. Soon afterwards, I became obsessed with the Catholic Church—perhaps because only the Catholics have saints, and if I was going to be one then I had better be a Catholic. Every day on my way home from school, I would tiptoe into the Catholic

Church near my house and after dipping my hand in the bowl of holy water at the entrance, like I had seen on television, I would kneel in one of the pews and pray. I loved the smell of the books and polished wood, the burning candles, the stone statues, and the stained glass. I wanted to be part of it.

Whenever I found a dead bird, I would get a shoebox and create a little coffin. After wrapping the bird in toilet paper, or whatever scraps of cloth I could find in my mother's sewing room, I would gently put it in the coffin. Then, being careful no one saw me, I would carry it into the church and lay it at the feet of the Catholic Jesus to be blessed. Sometimes I would even light a candle to guide the soul of the small creature back to heaven. Finally, I would carry the coffin outside, crawl behind the bushes surrounding the church, and dig a hole and bury the bird.

I begged my mother to let me convert, but she said not until I was sixteen. By then, however, I was obsessed with boys—birds and the Catholic Church long forgotten.

At eighteen, I became a Zen Buddhist and a beatnik. I gave away most of my belongings, wore only dark clothing, and spent hours staring mindlessly at a point somewhere in front of my nose. This life of purity and austerity was in total contradiction with my ongoing obsession with boys and did not last long.

Then I discovered folk music. I thought I could reach God through singing, possibly taking others with me into an altered state of consciousness. I was a good singer and this often resulted in male attention, which blurred the boundary between God and sex. Eventually, I became disillusioned with relationships. They were, by their very nature, limited.

I began to follow Swami Muktananda, an Indian guru who espoused celibacy. This temporarily cleared up some of the conflict, if only superficially. Plus, there was quite a bit of singing at the Swami's ashram.

At some point during my twelve years of meditating and chanting with the Swami, I converted to Judaism. I was convinced that I had been a rabbi in a past life, and I wanted to be Jewish again. After months of classes and immersion in the *Mikvah* (ritual bath for cleansing), I stood before the *Torah* (the Old Testament) and recited the passage about Ruth the Convert. It was as if some ancient, lost part of me had been reclaimed. This joy was short-lived, however, because every Jewish person I knew still considered me a *shiksa* (a non-Jewish female).

All this sounds absurd, I know, but after Swami Muktananda died, I started going to the Faith in God Spiritual Church and was eventually baptized. I had come full circle—although the Spiritists certainly do not resemble the Methodists of my childhood.

◦◦⊏⊐※⊏⊐◦◦

My Christian baptism took place in 1992 during the church anniversary on Memorial Day Weekend. This was the same year Filomena "Mely" Naces and her assistant, Trinidad, came from the Philippines.

We had all heard Connie describe herself as unworthy, the "rotten apple at the bottom of the barrel." After suffering from several serious illnesses from which she nearly died—and including twenty-two major surgeries—she was healed in three sessions with Rev. Marcos Orbito, a psychic surgeon who was visiting Nevada. After this, she started reading the Bible and traveling to the Philippines, where she assisted Rev. Orbito and Rev. Filomena Naces in their healing missions. Soon she was also hosting healers from the Philippines at her home in Nevada. Eventually, a simple shed in the backyard became a more elaborate structure for the American branch of the Faith in God Spiritual Church

In 1985, while assisting in the chapel of Rev. Filomena Naces in Pangasinan, Mely called Connie to come into the healing room. Connie described this experience in an article by Jaime T. Licauco, which was published in 1987 in *Mr. & Mrs.*, a Filipino magazine:

> "I thought something was wrong with one of the patients. I went near her. Without saying a word, Mely made a fist with her right hand, raised it in front of me, and suddenly struck the air towards me, as if to throw something at me. At the same time, she said in an authoritative voice: 'You'll do the healing on this patient.'
>
> "... I suddenly froze, and I felt as though water was doused all over my body. Although I was conscious of what was

happening. I was not exactly myself. Something in me had changed. I walked behind the healing table and faced the patient lying there. At that moment, I knew intuitively what to do and what healing was all about.

". . . I placed my hand on him, and Mely slapped my left hand three times so hard it hurt. Then I got the cotton and did the healing."

◦—◦═╬═◦—◦

I had gotten to know several of the regulars, especially Dottie, who often rode to church with me on Sundays. I would leave Berkeley about 6:00 A.M. and pick her up in Davis at 7:00. Dottie was African-American with dreads, and she worked at a public library in Sacramento. She was slightly overweight and often on a diet. This usually meant bringing her own food to Lemmon Valley, including low-fat yogurt smoothies and fresh fruit. She would never be forced to eat one of Connie's cheese and baloney on white bread sandwiches. Dottie had a picture on her refrigerator of a 400-pound woman in a tutu, who was balanced precariously on one foot, rather like an elephant doing a bizarre ballet. The caption said: "You will look like this, too, if you open the door to the refrigerator." Dottie also struggled with a fibroid tumor.

The weekend of the baptism, we took another woman, Nadine, with us. She had recently discovered a lump in her breast, and the doctor who performed the biopsy said she had cancer. It was one more illness in a long list of health problems. Nadine was scheduled for a mastectomy in seven weeks. The wait was necessary because she was a single mother on welfare and needed government approval. I felt sorry for her, and offered to take her to Reno for healing every Sunday for the six weeks preceding her surgery. I hoped she could avoid a mastectomy. Unfortunately, these efforts would prove useless, because she went ahead with surgery. Nadine had a young child and was not taking any chances.

Shortly after her mastectomy, Nadine called to let me know her doctor had performed a postsurgical biopsy of the removed breast tissue and had found *no trace of cancer.* He was mystified as to why the tumor was *not there*. Six months later, she denied having said this. Perhaps it was too painful to admit, even to herself, that she had lost her breast unnecessarily. Connie said Nadine had been healed by God during the time between her diagnosis and the surgery, but she lacked faith and could not accept her healing.

⚬⚬═══✳═══⚬⚬

We arrived early enough to put our tents up for the weekend, and then we joined the others in the church. When Connie took her seat, everyone began to sing along with a cassette playing on the tape deck—including Connie's small dog, Baby, who howled off-key from behind the altar.

> "He healed the blind man, walked on the water.
> He touched the lame man and he started walking.
> All his children should get together,
> For we need Jesus now more than ever."

Connie began to preach on one of her favorite subjects: the Holy Spirit as the Comforter left behind by Jesus for the support of humankind: "And I will pray to the Father, and he shall give you another Comforter who may abide with you forever." John 14:16. On this particular Sunday, Connie also read from I Corinthians 14:13: "For by one spirit are we all baptized into one body, whether we are Jews or Gentiles."

At the conclusion of the sermon, everyone stood up and held out their palms facing the bottles of water and other offerings on the altar. Slowly swaying in unison, we sang, "Have faith in God . . . Have faith in God. . . ."

⚬⚬═══✳═══⚬⚬

Johnnie, Mack, and I had been deemed worthy to receive the sacrament of baptism. Johnnie was a fiftyish, good-natured Italian man from San Francisco. I never got to know him very well because he spent most of his time chain-smoking in his sports car in the parking lot.

Mack was a former used car salesman, who had gotten involved with New Age philosophy after a contentious divorce. He was middle-aged, smelled like cigarettes and expensive cologne, and was promoting a self-improvement course called *Avatar*, a series of weekend seminars that promised participants they would learn to create their own reality, at will. Mack's hard-sell approach to Avatar reminded me of Werner Erhardt's est program, and I was quite skeptical as to its value. By strange coincidence, Erhardt had also sold cars before going on to create his own empire within the human potential movement of the 1970s and 1980s.

Mack wore loose-fitting, white shirts and drawstring yoga pants. This was some sort of costume related to an event he had recently attended called *The 11:11*. He said The 11:11 was an initiation involving the opening of Doorways, believed by some to be bridges between two different realities: the old one, which was anchored in duality, and the new evolutionary Spiral of Oneness.

On January 11, 1992, the first of eleven Doorways was opened. According to Mack, after the Eleventh Doorway is opened the Earth will become a planet made up entirely of energy. It will no longer exist as solid matter in the Third Dimension, but rather become solely Fifth Dimensional. Humans who have evolved sufficiently to enter through all of the eleven Doorways will become the etheric residents of this newly-formed realm. At the time, this sounded preposterous to me, but no stranger than the members of a certain Christian sect who are waiting for the "Rapture" when God will take them all to heaven, leaving the rest of us behind to be destroyed.

◦◦❖◦◦

I went first. As I knelt in front of the altar with Connie on one side and Mely on the other, Connie asked me seven questions regarding my understanding of the meaning of baptism and my commitment to the church. I vowed to incorporate the concept of universal brotherhood into my life and *act* on it. After reading from Ephesians, Connie dipped her forefinger in oil and made the sign of the cross in the center of my forehead. She also poured a small amount of water on the top of my head while Mely held the open Bible above me. It was an ancient ceremony, this anointing, and I felt the gravity of it.

I imagined invisible golden light streaming into the top of my head from the open book. It was slightly disorienting—as if I had gone *somewhere else* and then been forcefully thrown back into the present.

After Mack and Johnnie had also been baptized, we stood at the front of the room and led the congregation in singing "He Chose Me." Then we passed out small cups of the blessed water and everyone went outside to eat lunch and wait for their turn to be called back in for healing.

Other than the dramatic moment of baptism, my first meeting with Mely was unremarkable. She seemed to be focused almost entirely inward, and spoke little while she was in Lemmon Valley. She was deep water that ran strong, and her touch in the healing room was as gentle as the caress of a rose petal.

Later, I learned that psychic surgeons are vulnerable when they leave the Philippines and go abroad to do healing. Some people believe there is an energy field, or vortex, in the Philippines that is found in only a few other places on Earth, including Brazil. This field bridges the different dimensions of reality and strengthens the psychic power of the healers. Intense concentration is necessary while they are away from home. There are many theories about why the Philippine Islands are said to be one of several planetary centers of psychic phenomena. Some people believe they are the lost islands of Lemuria, a highly advanced civilization that was submerged millions of years ago. Others believe the healers are highly evolved, reincarnated souls from Atlantis.

That night when the festivities were over and everyone else was sleeping, I sat alone under the stars playing my guitar and singing softly. Mely approached out of the darkness and sat down next to me. After listening for awhile, she said, "Please come to the Philippines and sing for my church."

Thus, my destiny was set on a new and unexpected course.

The Philippines

The Fortune Cookie

Lawen mu pamu ing mallari, bayu ka matul.
Observe first before you make a decision.

I made the decision to go to the Philippines while eating lunch at "The Little Flower Chinese Restaurant" on Shattuck Avenue in Berkeley, California. I was taking a brief respite from a terribly boring legal secretary assignment, and this was the final day to get a cheap ticket for the particular week I wanted to travel. After four hours of typing subpoenas and talking on the phone with hysterical people who had been in auto accidents and only wanted to get what they had coming from their insurance companies, I realized I had to get out and breathe fresh air. I needed mental space.

As I walked to the Little Flower, a throng of U.C. Berkeley students rushed past me on their way to class. Lemmon Valley and the Faith in God Spiritual Church seemed far away. Manila seemed even further away from Shattuck Avenue and my safe and fairly predictable existence. Forty-six years old, and I had never been out of the United States, except to Mexico and briefly to Canada.

Ignoring the roar and fumes of the diesel buses, I passed the panhandlers lying on the sidewalk in front of the BART station, their noses, ears, and other body parts pierced with metal jewelry, many hauling their belongings in pilfered grocery carts. I passed the architectural magnificence of the Berkeley Public Library, the tiny shop where they sold cigars and ice cream, and the Multiplex Theatre. I entered the Little Flower. Settling into a quiet booth by myself at the back of the restaurant, I perused the *Daily Californian* absentmindedly. I was still mentally frozen regarding the decision that loomed large, but it had to be made before the travel agency closed at 5:00 P.M.

Chinese food is pretty much the same in restaurants everywhere. This is one certain thing in an uncertain world. I am grateful for

33

egg rolls, spicy soup with tofu, green beans, and delicately curled shrimp in garlic sauce. I am comforted by the ever-present cup of mildly-flavored jasmine tea and, at the end of the meal, a fortune cookie lying casually atop a check handed to me by a smiling waitress—actually, the *waiter* at the Little Flower was a refined, middle-aged Chinese man who had been a medical doctor before coming to America.

On this particular day in the fall of 1992, I took a deep breath and said a silent prayer as I reached for the cookie: *Please, God, let this cookie give me the answer. Should I go to the Philippines?* As I unfolded the tiny scrap of paper that would define the next chapter of my life, I took another deep breath and held it, suspended, for a long time as I read these words:

> A ONCE IN A LIFETIME ADVENTURE AWAITS YOU IN THE SOUTH PACIFIC ISLANDS.

The Miracle
and the Enigma

Albert Einstein said, "There are two views of life: either there are no miracles, or everything is a miracle." He also theorized that energy and matter are interchangeable: $E=MC_2$, which could be interpreted, within the context of psychic surgery, to mean that the physical body and the energy that animates the body arise from a common Divine source, referred to by many as *God*.

Antonio S. Araneta—a highly respected researcher into the subject of psychic surgery and the paranormal—is quoted as saying: "Just because your pattern of thinking cannot comprehend the phenomena, it does not mean that they do not exist. The most important thing is an open-minded approach. This is naturally hard to achieve, because no matter how open you think your mind is, it has probably been weakened, perhaps even atrophied, by years of confinement within a narrow pattern of thought. As soon as we begin to understand that energy and matter are interchangeable, we discover that not everything can be regarded as matter. There may be a fourth medium, not just solid, liquid, and gas. Viewed in this way, everything is possible." (6)

Continued on page 41.

The Airport and Manila

Say takot manlalpud ag pakakabat.
Fear springs from ignorance.

A few weeks later, I am sitting on my small suitcase outside of the baggage claim area in the Manila airport, hunched over almost in a fetal position. I am sweating profusely, even under my most flimsy cotton dress. The air is thick with humidity, and it is unbearably hot. I have just thrown away my only sweater in the ladies bathroom because I will not need it for the next two months.

The airport assaults my senses. The hordes of people in motion, the noise of a thousand voices, taxis, buses, cars, trucks, and airplanes, the exclamations of greeting and tears of departure; the very din of the place comes at me in waves and I am momentarily paralyzed.

"Miss, oh miss. You lost your sweater in the *comfort room* [bathroom]."

I look up and see a smiling brown face peering down at me, concern in her eyes.

"No, you keep it. I don't want it."

I continue staring at the floor, thinking about what a stupid idea it was to book a flight with a five-hour stopover in Seoul, Korea, where everything reeked of insecticide and there were hardly any chairs, and the police would not let anyone sit on the floor. The plane flies southwest over the Tropic of Cancer and the greenish-gray mountains of Japan: twenty-four hours in transit instead of a straight-through, seventeen-hour flight, with an additional stop in Hawaii to change planes and eat chocolate-covered macadamia nuts. After fish at four in the morning and a desperate attempt to sleep slumped over in the narrow seat, I have arrived, only to be overwhelmed by total chaos.

Someone taps lightly on my shoulder.

"Hello. Are you okay?"

I look up and see a familiar face. Well, not that I *know* the thirty-ish, blond-haired man standing over me, but he has white skin and speaks American English.

"I'm tired and don't know what to do."

"Do you have a hotel?"

"I'm scared to get into a taxi by myself."

"Ride with me to Pension Natividad. All the foreigners stay there. My name is Bill . . . from San Francisco."

Soon we are standing in front of the clerk at Pension Natividad. Bill offers to share a room with me to save money, but I am not willing to spend the night with a stranger. We each pay $20 for a private room, and then Bill goes his way and I go mine, grateful for the brief kindness of a fellow traveler.

Pension Natividad is set back from the busy street and has a shaded courtyard and garden. There is a small indoor restaurant with a limited menu that is served twice a day. The quiet hotel offers an opportunity to rest and digest the events of the past twenty-four hours.

Later, I lie nearly naked on a thin, foam mattress in the small room, directly under a ceiling fan that produces just enough moving air to cool my body to a tolerable temperature. Perhaps I will survive the swelter if I lie totally motionless. *How long does it take to become acclimated to such a severe change in temperature?* I wonder.

After a short, restless sleep, I "sign out" with the uniformed, rifle-carrying guard at the front gate, and find myself in the street outside of the tall barricade surrounding the hotel. It is about midnight. Actually, I do not know the exact time, only that I am hungry.

Pension Natividad is located at the southern end of the Ermita District, a popular tourist area filled with hotels, restaurants, souvenir and antique shops, airline ticket offices, and money-changers, who beckon from open shop doorways, shouting "Dollars. Dollars. Sell your dollars here."

Many of the well-known faith healers consult with groups of foreigners in the large hotels of the district. Ermita was also Manila's infamous "red-light district" until just before my arrival in early 1993, when the "girlie" bars were closed down, leaving dilapidated nightclubs with boarded-up doorways all along Mabini and del Pilar Streets.

There are people all around me as I walk through the streets of Manila for the first time, even though it is the middle of the night. The street lights are dimmed by about two-thirds because of an electrical power shortage. This is called a *brown-out*, as opposed to a *black-out*, when the electricity is turned off completely. The faded light is filtered through humid air, creating a thin haze that renders everything slightly surreal. It is like being in a dream sequence in a film. The people in the streets are shadows walking hurriedly with determination. Strangely enough, after my initial panic at the airport, this night scene is not frightening—perhaps because rape in the Philippines carries a possible death sentence.

———✳———

I am relieved to discover Rosie's Diner about five blocks from the hotel. Stepping through the front door is like taking a step back in time to 1950s America and the malt shop where I hung out in North Philly as a teenager. The cold breeze from the air-conditioner begins to envelop me, and I am able to think clearly for the first time since the plane landed. It is like coming out of anesthesia; the mental fog lifts and everything becomes brighter.

In the center of the diner is a horseshoe-shaped, Formica-topped counter surrounded by metal stools with red vinyl seats. The floor is made of shiny, black and white linoleum tiles, and high on the wall in a prominent position is a red neon sign announcing: "AL EATS HERE." There is also an advertisement for Coke. American rock and roll, circa 1970, pounds rhythmically from the jukebox.

Seated at the counter is a strange gathering of craggy, worn-out looking, mostly white men. They appear battered and rough, as if tossed up by the sea to flounder on a foreign shore. Many of them are scarred, and the bones in their faces seem somehow distorted, as if they had been broken and then healed at odd angles. These men are frightening, even under the bright lights of the diner. I take a seat at a table close to the counter to better observe them, and when I hear them speak with thick accents, it becomes obvious they are from Australia.

The menu is a twelve-page, clear plastic-enclosed folio requiring careful consideration. Each page is devoted to food from a different country. Written in the margins are indecipherable jokes and references to people who are most likely regular customers. After ordering eggs, fried potatoes, and coffee—because for me it is morning even though it is after midnight—I continue to watch the men seated at the counter. They are all smoking cigarettes and flirting with the waitresses. The place has the feel of a private club, and I almost expect to be thrown back out into the street because I am not a member.

While waiting for my food, I watch a pretty Filipina wearing a miniskirt and bright red lipstick approach one of the men at the counter. She is young and seems so innocent. Her round face, clear skin, and soft brown eyes form a stark contrast to the coarse features of the man. But, after a brief discussion, I am surprised when she leaves with him through a side door. I watch as they disappear up a tall staircase to the rooms above the diner. It finally occurs to me that she is a prostitute. Then I notice the diner is filled with beautiful young women flirting with the Australians.

I am in neutral mental space, a limbo outside of time under the fluorescent lights of the diner. A certain detachment and peacefulness comes over me when traveling alone in a foreign country. Most of the people around me cannot speak English, and I cannot speak their language, except regarding superficial things like ordering food in a restaurant or asking for a bathroom. It causes my interior dialogue to intensify. I experience acutely the boundary of my own flesh. My perception of the world and events around me is sharper, more focused. I become a self-contained unit without the distraction of conversation with others and the attendant responsibilities of human relationships. I have no censor, no supervision, and very little sense of shame. I want to go running, flying naked through the hot Manila streets, past the hordes of humanity in motion, the poor huddled under cardboard boxes clustered on the sidewalks, the children wide-eyed staring, the smells of cooking and garbage, the thick, black exhaust from the thousands of vehicles clogging the streets, the putrid stink of urine spilling forth from stained doorways, and the smell of burning kerosene spewing from portable generators in front of the shops during times of limited electricity.

The city is vast and intimidating. Just a few blocks from my hotel is the sparkling business district of Makati, with its glamorous Western-style shopping and upscale dining and entertainment. But Makati is farther away than I am able to venture. Dizzy and disoriented, I sleep long hours and then walk the streets of Ermita trying to get used to being in a foreign country. After three days, I am ready to leave for Pangasinan Province.

The Miracle
and the Enigma

It has been postulated that the psychic surgeons have the ability to manipulate the electromagnetic force fields that hold the physical universe, including the human body, in solid form. Jaime Licauco, a Filipino researcher who has studied and written extensively on the subject of psychic surgery, explains it thus:

"The healers form a strong etheric force, or energy, in their hands through intense concentration. This energy penetrates matter at the cellular or even subatomic levels, where matter and energy are interchangeable [and allows the healer to remove tumors and diseased tissue]."

Licauco goes on to say: "The natural magnetic force of the cells enables them to return to their normal formation after the healer takes his hands out of the body; therefore, no trace of incision or surgery will be seen." (7)

Some people believe psychic surgery works by temporarily reversing the electric polarity of living cells. Imagine the body is like a glass of water. When you slip your finger into the water, the molecules of the water separate to make room for your finger, and when you remove your finger, the water fills in the space left behind.

Continued on page 46.

Pangasinan: Dust in the Land of Salt

Siasino man nga mangapput, ti lapayagna ti ikis ti napanglaw
Isu umkis to met ket, saan to nga maipangag.
*He who shuts his ears to the cries of the poor will also cry
and will not be heard.*

"What will you do in Pangasinan?" asks my host, Ricky Abalos.

I have been asking myself this same question since leaving the States. I smile and give a simple response: "Play guitar and sing at the Faith in God Spiritual Church."

Ricky lives in Berkeley. A friend introduced us because she knew we were planning to visit the Philippines at the same time. He is curious about faith healing, and has volunteered to pick me up in Manila and drive me to Mely's in the rural community of Vacante so he can experience it for himself. A ride in a private car is certainly easier than negotiating public transportation out of Manila. We are planning to spend Saturday night at his family's beach house in San Fabian on the Gulf of Lingayen.

We are traveling in a large van with Ricky's younger brother, Benny, and a chiropractor from California and his Filipino wife. I met them in Manila when I sought relief for neck pain caused by the long flight. He is eager to learn about his new wife's culture, including the faith healers he has heard so much about.

Insulated from the chaos of the city by tinted glass, the hum of the air conditioner, and soft music playing on the radio, the van carries us through densely populated streets filled with school children wearing blue and white uniforms hurrying to class. We pass the gated communities of the wealthy and then cross the Pasig River, which is filled with floating garbage and lined with squatters' shacks, their laundry drying in the wind. After miles of overcrowded slums, we are finally rolling north on the MacArthur Highway. But even here, outside of the city, the road is crowded with speeding buses, private cars, and an occasional handmade, wooden wagon with large wheels drawn by water buffalos with enormous curved horns. These work animals are also called *carabao*. Many of the wagons are covered with traditional woven baskets being taken to market.

The roads are also crowded with jeepneys, a uniquely Filipino method of transportation. At the end of World War II, the U.S. Army released the surplus jeeps left behind in the Philippines, and the Filipinos converted them into passenger vehicles by lengthening the bodies. Jeepneys typically have room for several passengers next to the driver and two rows of inward-facing seats running the length of the vehicle. The seats are always full and the aisles crowded. Jeepneys are often decorated with hood ornaments, mirrors, brightly-colored paintings, and humorous or religious slogans. There is usually a picture or statue of Jesus on the dashboard.

Jeepneys are similar to the "art cars" found in some places in the U.S., and reflect the creativity and individuality of their owners. New jeepneys are now manufactured in the Philippines, and about half of the jeepneys in the country are in Manila. They follow established routes, which are posted on the front of the vehicle, and make regular stops, much like buses. Fares are charged according to how far you ride, averaging five to ten cents for short distances.

Our journey takes us through the southern part of the wide plain that runs north/south through the center of Luzon, the largest of the Philippine islands. The view out the window is serene, with verdant rice fields and the wild mountains beyond.

Without warning, the van comes to an unexpected halt. A swarm of people cloaked in a fine, white dust has surrounded it, preventing us from continuing. The dust forms a cloud so thick it resembles fog.

There is a thin woman standing on the other side of the window from where I sit. She is straining her neck to see inside the van, but she cannot see me because of the tinted windows, although I can see her. She seems hopeful, but also confused, as if she is in shock. She makes an attempt to smile at the person she imagines sitting on my side of the window, but her smile never quite reaches the corners of her mouth. Her head is wrapped in a long white scarf partially shielding her face from the dust. The rest of her clothing is torn and stained. Slowly, she raises one of her outstretched hands in the direction of the window. Her eyes continue to stare, reflecting despair.

Suddenly, I realize she and the others surrounding the van are refugees from the devastation caused by Mt. Pinatubo. They have stopped us because they hope we will give them money. Ricky gets out of the van, stands in the middle of the crowd, and passes out several pesos to each person—in 1993, one U.S. dollar equaled approximately twenty-six pesos, so the gift of even a few pesos was significant.

Mt. Pinatubo, a volcano that had been dormant for 600 years, exploded violently in June 1991 and again in September 1992. Those who were not killed immediately were killed by *lahar*, a mixture of rain and ash that flowed down the hillsides into the fertile valleys at gale-force speed, wiping out entire villages. Lahar continues to flow each year during the rainy season, silting the rivers, causing flooding, and destroying the rice fields, farmlands, and fishponds.

The seismic activity of Mt. Pinatubo displaced approximately 1.5 million people and killed over 1,000. The eruptions also destroyed Clark Air Force Base, which closed abruptly, causing further economic devastation to the surrounding area. Many villagers moved to Manila, but others refused to leave their land. They continue to try different crops, hoping to find one that can be grown in the tainted soil. They also harvest before the rainy season, when the lahar begins to flow again.

Soon we are driving in Pangasinan Province, a crescent-shaped area bounded by the Zambales mountain range to the west and the Cordilleras to the east. The province extends to the rice paddies and sugarcane fields of Tarlac in the south, and to the Lingayen Gulf in the north, with its famed Hundred Islands National Park and the South China Sea.

Pangasinan means "land of salt" or "place where salt is made." The province has been given this name because one of the main occupations of the people in the coastal villages is making salt from sea water. The sun evaporates the water from salt ponds laid out at the edge of the sea, leaving behind yellowish, coarse salt crystals that contain an abundance of minerals and taste slightly sweet. Many rural Filipinos use this raw salt, although people in the cities increasingly want the more processed variety.

We reach the beach cottage late in the evening, and after a dinner of milk fish (*bangus*), rice, and fresh tomatoes, everyone goes to bed. I am filled with anticipation and am unable to sleep, so I lie down and listen to the ocean surf just outside the window until nearly sunrise.

The Miracle
and the Enigma

The understanding of psychic surgery has been developing for a long time and, hopefully, will continue to develop. In a speech given before the Philippine Medical Association in 1983, Dr. Jesus Lava quoted Harold S. Burr, a Professor of Anatomy at Yale University, who spoke in 1935 about the discovery of an *energy body:*

"[There is] a second body possessed by human beings, which provides a blueprint for the physical body, controlling and determining the function of cells and organs, and the shape, size, and colour of the physical body. This energy body is, in turn, affected by the emotions and mind of the individual." (6)

The energy body referred to by Professor Burr is more commonly known as the *aura.* Psychic surgeons and other energy healers usually work within the fifth layer of the aura, the *etheric body,* in order to effect change that can, in turn, result in physical healing.

Continued on page 51.

The Woman on the Roof

⊶⊰⊱✳⊰⊱⊷

Pasangvayem daguiti sangsangaili.
Welcome the stranger.

Awake at dawn to the crowing of a rooster, I leave the cottage quietly and walk out to the empty beach in my bare feet. Ricky and the others are still asleep. The smell of the early morning air is crisp and fresh—the sea placid and as smooth as a pane of glass. A few birds standing at the edge of the water observe me indifferently as I cautiously put my foot in the South China Sea for the first time. Much to my surprise, it is warm, not like the Pacific Ocean in Northern California, where the water is cold.

Soon I am walking aimlessly down the beach, but this is like no other beach I have ever walked on, because I am thousands of miles from the familiar. It reminds me of the movie *Prince of Tides*, when the three children run and leap off the end of a fishing dock holding hands, falling through green water, except I am alone on an empty beach walking, falling towards myself, falling towards the unknown.

Ahead is a sidewalk—no, it is a concrete road without curbs—jutting out into the sand, stopping abruptly. It invites me, and I turn towards it, leaving the sea behind. The air begins to smell of wind in dry grass, cooking fires, and flowering plants.

Nipa huts line the one-lane road. This is the first time I have seen this type of house, except in pictures in a travel guidebook. One hut has an open stall at the edge of the road, and it appears to be a food store because there are cellophane bags filled with chips and something that looks vaguely like string beans hanging from the roof. There is also a dirty, wooden table covered with lidded aluminum pots, probably for holding cooked food. Above, hang bunches of bananas and a rusty sign advertising cold drinks. The proprietor is nowhere to be seen.

The traditional nipa huts of the rural villages are simple structures that can be built in a couple of days. These dwellings are supported by wooden posts, and they are often elevated several feet off the ground to provide ventilation and prevent flooding during the rainy season. This also keeps out small rodents. The floor is usually made of split bamboo slats spaced about one-half inch apart, also for ventilation. A ladder that can be raised and lowered is used to enter the structure, or there may be more permanent wooden steps.

The materials used to build a nipa hut are usually found locally: bamboo poles and nipa (dried grass), wood, or siding made from split bamboo. These materials are lashed or woven together to keep the interior watertight. The roof is usually made of thatched nipa. The lightness of these dwellings prevents injury to the inhabitants if the house is toppled by an earthquake or typhoon. There are modern variations on the nipa hut, and some Filipinos build more substantial houses made of concrete.

∘∘⊏⊏✹⊐⊐∘∘

Although I am barefoot and the road is filled with irritating pebbles, curiosity forces me onward until I come to an enormous building—a church, yes it *is* a church—standing somewhat forlornly in the middle of the jungle. It is still quite early, and there is no one around except for a few sleepy dogs who bark at my arrival.

The building seems worn by rain and time. It definitely needs to be painted. There are eight oblong windows, but they are without glass—as if the builders ran out of money when they got to the windows. There are also several significant cracks in the cement walls.

Stepping off the road onto the grass, I look into one of the windows and see a wooden crucifix at least twelve by six feet hanging high on the wall at the front of the sanctuary. This Jesus does not welcome, however. He looks sad and tired, and also in need of fresh paint.

The floor at the front of the room is covered with faded, red carpet holding chairs laid out neatly in rows. The rest of the church has a hard-packed dirt floor with regular wooden pews. There is not a soul to be seen. The church is completely empty. I stand there for some time leaning on the window sill, until I hear an odd noise.

Turning toward the sound, I am amazed to see two turkeys *in flagrante delicto* six inches from my feet.

Startled and a bit embarrassed, although no one else is watching, I leave and walk around to the front of the building. Just then, a bell begins to ring, and children wearing school uniforms come running from every direction toward the front courtyard. They quickly form several lines and stand at attention. Music begins to play over a loudspeaker as several flags are raised up a pole, and the children sing along enthusiastically, while holding one hand to their foreheads. The song sounds like both a hymn and a national anthem, and this rather military ritual strikes me as a curious combination of church and state, something that might not be allowed in the U.S. When the music stops, the children march solemnly into the church.

I am still standing there taking all this in, when a young woman walks up to me.

"Hello, Miss. Welcome to San Fabian. Are you a visitor? Are you from the U.S.?"

"Yes," I say, nodding my head.

"Would you like a tour? If you are looking for the healer, he is not here."

This reminds me that Eleuterio Terte, the first healer in modern times to perform psychic surgery, was born in San Fabian. Perhaps she thinks I am looking for him, but I already know he is no longer alive.

She does not take me into the church, but rather leads me around to the far side of the building, where there is a wide, outside staircase leading up to the roof. We speak very little as we climb—because the stairs are steep and we are strangers and she does not know much English, nor I her language.

We are almost to the top, when there is a flapping noise to my left. Startled, I turn quickly and look through an open window into the sanctuary just in time to see a dozen birds fly out of the carved, wooden hair on the head of Jesus. They have made their nests on him and the rafters above. I am just at eye level with him at this point on the staircase, as he hangs there in perpetual agony for the sins of humankind. From this viewpoint, his head is almost as large as my entire body, and he is covered with cobwebs. Fortunately, he is not looking in my direction. That would be just too much.

Leaving Jesus behind, we arrive at the large, mostly flat roof of the church. Although it is only about 7:00 A.M., the sun has already risen in the sky, and it is beginning to get warm. The woman leads me to a small garden area with potted plants, a fishpond with live fish, and a bubbling fountain. She smiles reassuringly, as if there is nothing unusual about having a garden with a pond and a fountain on the top of a building. As I sit on a small wrought-iron bench at the edge of the pond, she hovers around me, friendly and eager to please.

Casually pointing, she turns my attention to a large wooden box with a glass door at one side of the garden. It is about as big as a piano box. Looking through the glass, I cannot believe my eyes. Inside it is a beautiful woman dressed in a formal evening gown. She appears to be made of wax. I want to put my hand on the glass to see if the box is refrigerated, but somehow I already know it is cold, even without touching it, because somewhere there is the faint hum of a motor. Also, perhaps this is something I do *not* really want to know, because it occurs to me that she is an *embalmed* woman, a *real* woman, a much-loved woman who died and was put here so her family could sit in the garden and talk to her as if she is still alive.

I look back at my hostess. I do not want to be considered rude, but I am in a panic from the strangeness of it all. So, after a quick "thank you," I run down the stairs, through the village, along the beach, and back to the cottage. Ricky and the others are just getting up and beginning to wonder where their guest from America has gone. I tell them only that I went to the beach. The servants bring us breakfast, and I eat in silence, pondering the events of the morning.

The Miracle
and the Enigma

Animism and The Roots of Psychic Surgery (8)

Perhaps the earliest account of what might be called "faith healing" in the Philippines comes from the chronicles of Antonio Pigafetta in his book *The First Voyage Around the World*. (9) Pigafetta describes Magellan and his party arriving in Cebu in 1521, where they observed unusual healings. Magellan brought Christianity in the form of Catholicism to the Philippines, and towards the end of the nineteenth century, Spiritism was also introduced.

Filipino faith-based healing and psychic surgery are based on Christianity and traditional *animistic* beliefs. The word *animism* is derived from the Latin word *anima*, meaning *breath* or *soul*. Another term for animism, which may be more familiar to modern readers, is *shamanism*. Animistic beliefs are among the oldest human beliefs, most likely dating from the Stone Age. The basic tenet of animism is that spirit exists in everything, living and inanimate, including animals, trees, rocks, and water. The individual soul, whether beneficial, neutral, or malicious, was believed to reincarnate over and over again.

Continued on page 56.

The Church at Vacante: Getting There

Bisan ngain an tadong, mauli ha kalugaringon.
Wherever a man goes, in the end he comes home.

"Do you have to take your clothes off? Does it hurt? Will there be *real* blood?"

Benny Abalos is only a small boy, ten years old, with large, brown eyes and hair carefully spiked with sweet-smelling pomade, but he voices our collective questions.

"The healer will move aside your clothing, but if a person is very sick they might have to take off their clothes. When I had psychic surgery in the U.S. it didn't hurt, and there may be blood."

"Do they put their hands in you? Does it cost money?"

The healer will put her hands inside of your body, although some people think she only touches the skin. There is no charge, but you can give a donation."

"But, Miss Bryan, Do *I* have to have it done to *me*?"

"No one will force you, Benny."

The boy stares at me with a vacant expression, as if he is turning this information over in his mind and trying to understand it.

After about forty miles on the busy road leading from San Fabian to the village of Binalonan, we rejoin the MacArthur Highway for a brief distance. Just past a large sign proclaiming "REGION I: HOME OF CITIZEN-FRIENDLY POLICEMEN" in bright red letters, we turn onto a narrow, gravel road bordered by both nipa huts and more sturdy structures. The road is filled with tricycles. These brightly-decorated vehicles are small motorcycles to which a rear cart has been attached. The cart is designed to seat up to three

52

adult passengers, plus multiple shopping bags, but often there are as many as eight adults and children crowded into and sometimes hanging from the sides of a tricycle. Dust from the dry road swirls around the drivers and their passengers as they maneuver wildly past each other in a race to and from the main highway.

I look out the window and watch as we pass each house, thinking *is this where Mely lives?* After about twenty minutes on the bumpy, pothole-filled road, we round a sharp curve and the van comes to an abrupt halt at the front gate of the Faith in God Spiritual Church. As we descend into the humid air, Mely greets us with the traditional Filipino greeting "Mabuhay," which means "long life," but also "hello," "goodbye," and "good luck." She looks deeply into my eyes and gives me a warm hug. I can hardly believe the whispered invitation she extended weeks ago has resulted in my being here.

The house and the church are constructed of cement blocks, and the entire front yard of the house is filled with potted orchids of every hue. Some are in baskets hanging gracefully from trees. It is lush and welcoming, and everywhere I look there are smiling, brown faces. We have arrived just as many other people are also arriving for the 9 A.M. service. After passing along a line of elderly gentlemen, each of whom politely averts his gaze while shaking my hand, we are ushered into the church.

Faded, green-flowered linoleum covers the floor, and decorations from a previous Christmas are still in evidence. The crepe paper flowers hanging from the ceiling flutter gently in the breeze from an electric fan. Hanging plants are framed in the open windows, and although the sun is already blazing outside, the concrete building holds the coolness of the previous night.

First there are introductory prayers and several songs from the choir—some in nearly indecipherable English and some in the native language, which is a mixture of Pangasinese and Tagalog, a language spoken mainly in the large cities of the Philippines.

The choir sits directly across the aisle from me. Consisting mostly of young women, their voices blend in sweet harmony. Somewhere in the back of the room, a baby wails every fourth note in perfect time with the songs. An old man is playing a guitar that is terribly out of tune. Later inspection will reveal the strings to be ordinary wire from the hardware store. Unfortunately, the wire is strung on a classical guitar, resulting in a warped neck that can never be properly tuned, and the sound of the instrument is doomed to be forever flawed. But nothing dampens the liveliness of the singers or the musician. The entire congregation is one musical body with a palpable presence.

Turning my head to the right, I am stunned to see an incredibly beautiful man sitting several rows behind me. He has thick black hair, white teeth, and high cheekbones. An inner radiance shines from his face. He exudes sweetness, but also strength and confidence, as if he knows his exact place in the perfect order of things. He is wearing a blue tee-shirt imprinted with the words "I Love New York."

Mely and several other women sit in a line against the wall to the left of the podium. A similar line of men sits to the right. The women are wearing simple dresses, low-heeled shoes, and nylon stockings, and the men, starched white shirts and pressed polyester slacks. These people at the front seem rather somber, but fortunately their seriousness is tempered by the singing of the choir. During the lengthy service, they take turns preaching. The tone of their voices is dramatic, and they make frequent references to the Bible, which is lying on the podium before them.

Mely is the only one who does not preach. She sits quietly and seems almost invisible. In spite of my enthusiasm about finally making it to my destination, it all seems a bit dreary, in part because I am tired and do not understand the language.

After several people have spoken, Mely rises from her chair and formally introduces me to the congregation. Moving to the front and taking out my guitar, I sing "Michael Row the Boat Ashore" and "Amazing Grace." The congregation smiles with approval and Mely beams with pride. *Mr. I Love New York* stares at me, swaying slightly to the sound of my voice.

At the conclusion of the service, several people wait in the back of church for Mely to begin healing. But first she goes next door for lunch with the family and several guests. *Mr. I Love New York* stands quietly in a corner of the living room, and even with all the conversation and introductions, I am aware of him observing me. After a few minutes, Mely introduces us. His name is Joseph, and he is her brother. I cannot remember now what we spoke about, only that we could not stop staring at each other.

After lunch, Mely returns to the church. Strangely enough, after their initial curiosity about psychic surgery, my entourage from Manila says little and quickly leaves for home. Perhaps the midday heat has made them sleepy.

Mely's healing room is located at the back of the sanctuary near the front door and the office. The tiny room is furnished with only a chair and a rectangular, wooden table covered with a plastic tablecloth. The faint odor of burnt coconut oil fills the room. There is a wooden box with a small hole in the lid hanging on the wall. Money is put through the hole so no one can see how much is given, preventing possible embarrassment on the part of the person making the donation.

I wait with the others, and when my turn comes I enter the healing room and close the door. Trinidad, Mely's assistant, tells me to take off my clothes and get on the table. Like Connie, Mely appears to be in some sort of trance. As I climb onto the table, I am once again filled with expectation, but also a twinge of anxiety. I do not understand why I am frightened. Am I afraid nothing will happen? Is it the simple fear of surrendering to the unknown?

Her touch is light and tender. There is no heavy thrusting or dramatic tumor removal. I am still waiting for a miracle when she is finished, but somehow I no longer care, because I am floating in bliss from the energy that flows from her hands. My nervousness has evaporated, and I am light and filled with peace.

The Miracle and the Enigma

In the animistic belief system, the indwelling souls, or spirits, were called *Anitos*. The term also included the higher Gods, evil spirits, beneficial spirits of lower rank, and the spirits of people who had died. *Anito* can be further defined as an entity possessing superior intelligence, but lacking a corporeal (physical) body.

Each type of Anito had a specific purpose. There were the *Mangmangkik,* who lived in the forest, and from whom the woodcutter asked permission to cut trees. Some Anitos captured human bodies at the time of death. For this reason, the bodies of the dead were watched over closely before they were buried. The *Kata-taoan* could make themselves invisible or take human form, sometimes in the form of giants. They possessed boats that traveled like balloons in the air. Perhaps the *Kata-taoan* can be viewed as evidence of visits to Earth by travelers from other solar systems.

Continued on page 64.

Village Life

Sa kayano, anaa ang katahum.
In simplicity there is beauty.

Filipino families tend to be large, making it difficult to remember all the names and interconnected relationships. There are six households in the Naces family compound. Besides Mely, three other families live in sturdy houses made of concrete: Mely's sister, Belen, her brother Joseph, and Lucy and her two-year-old daughter. Lucy's husband works in Saudi Arabia and only comes home to visit once a year at Christmas. As is the case with many Filipino families, poverty often forces one family member to work overseas and send money back to support the others.

The nipa hut behind the church has a sign over the door written in a childish hand that says: "Mely's House." This hut has two rooms, each about ten by ten feet. I sleep in one room and the other is empty. I have only a chair and a bed covered with a mosquito net. I lie in bed at night and watch the geckos that scurry on the walls. Sometimes they fall on the net above me. Small domestic animals sleep under the raised structure; the carabao and pigs are kept in adjacent pens.

Buyat, his wife, and their two children, Minchu and Bernard, live in a nipa hut on the other side of the irrigation ditch running along one side of the church. Buyat works with Joseph in the fields. I assume this family is quite poor because they are all thin and the children seem sickly.

Mely's house is on the other side of the church, and there is another nipa hut next to it that sits about twelve feet up in the air on posts. Although I have never seen a ladder to access this dwelling, there must be one, because there is always a tiny, ancient woman sitting in the open doorway, a diminutive Buddha smoking a cigar.

Mely's mother died when she was young, leaving her father to raise several children, most of them girls. He remarried and had a second family, also girls. Although it is difficult to keep track of all these "sisters," Luna is memorable. She lives about a mile down the road with her mother. When Luna was only five years old, one of the foreigners who came to visit Mely, a man from Germany, became so enamored of her physical beauty that he tried to adopt her. Luna speaks excellent English and is good at translation.

Luna once lived in Manila, where she worked six days a week, ten hours a day making shoes on an assembly line. Her salary was only $25 per week, but she supported herself and also sent money home to her family. Luna's dream is to marry an American and become a lawyer.

⊶⊷✳⊶⊷

Almost every morning, the women gather on the cement patio at the back of Mely's house to wash clothes. A single pump provides cold water, and everyone takes turns pumping it into large plastic washtubs. There is much scrubbing and rinsing, but this is also a time for gossip. The sound of their sing-song voices washes over me as I clean my clothes.

A flush toilet and cement shower stall are located adjacent to the laundry area. Mely is considered well-to-do because she has a modern toilet. No one but those of us in her immediate household and visitors on Sunday are allowed to use it. Thinking about it now, I have no memory of any other toilets or outhouses in the entire compound. Perhaps they all used Mely's facilities at night when no one was looking.

Once a day, Trinidad helps me heat water on the propane stove in the kitchen for bathing. I carry the hot water out to the shower. Bathing is complicated and involves multiple buckets and combining water of differing temperatures, but it only becomes really difficult when I need to wash shampoo out of my hair.

Occasionally, a young woman arrives with a small suitcase containing fingernail polish and the usual accoutrements: nail files and cutters, brushes, cuticle softener, and hand cream. The neighborhood women gather on a side porch in the afternoon to have their nails "done." Sleepy from the midday heat, small children curl up in any available lap.

The Naces family, with its extended circle of friends and relatives, lives a mutually supportive, tribal lifestyle. They gather for no particular purpose other than to relax in each other's company and talk about the weather, who got married or had a fight, and whatever other aspects of daily life seem important at the moment. Actually, I have no idea what they are talking about most of the time because of the language barrier. But I find these to be the best times, the most relaxing times, when I float on a current of soft, melodious voices and forget my troubles, which no longer seem quite so important. It is a feeling of being totally in the moment—no past, no future—only the lightness of *now*. It is ordinary and rich.

⚬⚬◁▪▪▪✳▪▪▪▷⚬⚬

My private time with Mely is in the morning. Like all relationships, we discover each other in small pieces, often as we sip our coffee at the kitchen table. She does not tell much of her own story. When we are together, I do most of the talking. She is a mirror that reflects me back onto myself, like a good psychotherapist. Mely is my muse, gliding silently through the house in her blue slippers and faded flowered housedress.

Although she is enigmatic and elusive, Mely is aware of everything that goes on in the family and church community. She wields power and influence, as evidenced by the many people who come to her for advice. I watch them as they sit in the front parlor, speaking in hushed, serious tones. The discussion often revolves around someone who is sick or dying, or in some sort of trouble. Sometimes, they bring the ill person with them for healing. This is on Tuesdays and Thursdays, if it is not a Sunday. They always seem relieved when they leave. There is no charge, but usually a donation of pesos is given, or perhaps a bag of rice, a chicken, or fresh vegetables.

Blending into the current of daily life in Vacante is natural and easy. First, there is breakfast: instant coffee or Lipton tea, thick with canned, evaporated milk and raw sugar, fresh eggs with bright yokes, and rice, which is served at every meal. The food choices for lunch and dinner are limited to fish or chicken, fruit, and greenish-gray vegetables. I never know what vegetables are being served because they are always mashed and flavored to such a degree that their original form is impossible to discern. At some point, Trinidad concludes that Americans like French fries, and she begins cooking them every night as an alternative to rice.

◦◦⊂⊏❋⊐⊃◦◦

A week later, I am ready to take a tricycle to the nearest village, Binalonan, which is too small to be listed in most of the tourist guidebooks. Binalonan has a doctor's office, a combination pharmacy/card shop, a fertilizer and feed store, and a place to buy tires and other car parts. The small food market is busy only on Fridays, when people come from miles around to sell their wares.

After wrapping my head in a scarf to avoid the ever-present dust of the road, I stand in front of the house until a tricycle screeches to a halt in front of me. I am acutely aware of being larger than everyone else as they move aside to make room for me. After giving the driver the required fare, three pesos, we are rolling down the road toward town. The other passengers politely look away and no one speaks, but I am content to be ignored and enjoy the cool breeze on my face.

After about twenty minutes, the tricycle arrives in "downtown" Binalonan, and I descend with the others into the mid-morning sun. Looking down the unpaved main street, everything shimmers from the intense heat like a mirage on a desert horizon. I wonder how I will survive long enough to buy groceries.

Although I have already decided to take the jeepney to the larger village of Urdaneta, about 15 miles away, a sign over a doorway catches my eye: "Place of Beauty." Curious, I venture in and discover it is a hair salon, but there are no customers. The employees, several young girls, seem lethargic and bored.

Without thinking too much about it, I impulsively decide to get a perm. I am able to communicate this by taking several curlers from a basket and making twirling motions around my head. The women in the shop begin a flurry of activity, and soon I am sitting in a straight-backed, wooden chair while they apply the stinking, ammonia-laced solution to my hair one strand at a time and roll it up into curlers.

After about thirty minutes of glancing through what appears to be a Filipino movie star magazine, the perm solution has seeped through the curlers and is beginning to burn into my scalp. Just as I reach the point where I cannot take it any longer, one of the women says it is time to wash out the solution.

However, they do not have running water. It has to be carried in from somewhere else. Barely tepid, they deliver the water in stages as I sit with my head hanging over a bucket. After rinsing, the curlers are removed and my hair is blow-dried. I am looking pretty good when I emerge from the Place of Beauty, but I would not recommend getting a perm in the rural Philippines.

◦◦◁▣✳▣▷◦◦

Back out in the street, I locate the appropriate corner and board a southbound jeepney. Speeding down the MacArthur Highway once again, I welcome the "air-conditioning" produced by the wind, even though it is dirty from the burning of poorly-refined gasoline. Following the Filipino custom, I cover my nose with a cloth hanky to avoid choking on the fumes.

The jeepney drops me off in front of the centrally-located market in Urdaneta. Like Manila, the chaos of the street hits me viscerally with such force that I sway on my feet and nearly fall over backwards. Quickly slipping into an opening between two fast-food booths at the edge of the sidewalk, I enter the interior of the market. The feeling here is subdued. There are only a few shoppers, and the clerks seem sleepy. They sit fanning themselves, rising only when a customer indicates interest in making a purchase.

Wandering down a narrow walkway between the many different booths in the dry goods section, I peruse cotton sheets, towels, and dishrags stacked high on large tables. Another table holds men's jeans, shirts, socks, and underwear. A colorful blaze of mostly polyester women's clothing hangs from the ceiling; below are piles of ten-dollar batik dresses from Indonesia and women's underwear, none of it large enough to fit me.

I meander down row after row, passing piles of merchandise for children: toys of every description, diapers, and lacy confirmation dresses in plastic protective wrapping. I gag from the smell of mothballs when I pass the cheap leather goods. There are watches and wedding rings, pots and dishes, and plastic items in abundance, much of it made in China and of poor quality. Few tourists come to this part of the Philippines, and the economy is poor. Many of the local people live at a subsistence level, which is reflected in the goods for sale.

Moving on, I reach the noisy grocery and fresh food areas. The smell of ripe mangoes beckons, and I buy a large bag of them. There are long, wooden tables holding avocados, papaya, bananas, pineapples, foot-long string beans, potatoes, and other vegetables I have never seen before. Soon I am carrying enough fresh food to last for several days.

I purchase a cup of freshly roasted peanuts, salty and coated in delicately-flavored oil for five pesos, and snack on them as I continue to browse. Moving towards the packaged food in the grocery section, I buy a dozen eggs, which are handed over in a thin, plastic sack, to be carefully guarded against breakage. Bulk items are stacked everywhere: laundry soap, pot scrubbers, toilet paper, rice, beans, sugar, salt, canned milk, instant coffee, tea bags, crackers, cookies, and chips.

Drops of perspiration begin to bead up and run down the middle of my back and under my arms and breasts as I struggle to carry my purchases while eating the peanuts. But soon I am in the fish section, and I *must* have some milkfish. These shimmering silver, delicately-flavored fish are the local favorite, and I buy two pounds of them. Shrimp, mussels, and strange slimy things that look like they might be eels are offered for sale. The poultry section is located between the fish and meat. Some of the chickens have already been butchered and are lying on the counter; some are still alive and squawking in wooden cages.

My relaxed exploration of the Urdaneta market begins to change when I reach the edge of the meat section and am hit by the smell that rises in waves from the decaying flesh. It is acrid, slightly rancid, the odor further intensified by the heat. A sudden wave of nausea overwhelms me. This is definitely not Whole Foods or Safeway, where everything is wrapped neatly in plastic, clearly labeled, and stored in immaculate, refrigerated cases. Here, unidentifiable animal parts lie openly atop cement counters. The edges of some of the bloody pieces are dried out and beginning to curl and darken.

Women wearing oilcloth aprons and rubber gloves sit behind the counters swatting absentmindedly at the clouds of flies gathered around the meat. There are troughs with hoses and running water behind the displays, presumably so everything can be washed clean at night.

Suddenly, I am acutely aware that all of this is about killing—about eating and being eaten. Clutching my purchases tightly, I leave the market. On the way home, I seriously consider the possibility of becoming a vegetarian.

The Miracle
and the Enigma

Minor deities included the *Litao*, who sometimes appeared as cats with eyes of fire that might be transformed into frightening giants. *Pugot* lived in buildings that were unoccupied or under construction. The *Al-alia* were the ghosts of dead persons. There were the *Kaibaan*, dwarfs who dwelt in ant-hills, and the *Bagba-gutot*, who lived in shrubs.

Some Anitos protected warriors; others prevented against disease. They were responsible for weather, plant growth, and good health. Illness was deemed punishment for offending the Anitos.

Charms were used to bring good luck and ward off possible evil. Ritual, worship, and sacrifice were necessary to pacify these spirits. A wide variety of goods was offered, according to the particular Anito being appealed to and the severity of the need. Rituals were presided over by *Managanito*, priestesses who invoked oracles and idols, and interpreted dreams and omens, in order to determine the best time to take any particular action, such as the planting of crops.

Continued on page 68.

The Wake

Ang honi tambal so Masulob-ong kasing-kasing.
Music is the medicine of a lonely heart.

I have been in Vacante for only a few days, when early one evening we set out for a distant *barrio* to attend the wake of someone who has died. The choirgirls are wearing their Sunday clothes: clean-pressed flowered shirts, dark-colored skirts, and sandals. They are somber as they pile into the jeepney and sit with their music books in their hands, the usual laughter and chatter strangely missing.

After about forty minutes over narrow roads, and finally to a road that is not really a road at all, but sun-baked ruts through an empty field, we come to a stop and everyone climbs out of the jeepney. It is silent except for the whisper of insects. Single file down a narrow path, crossing an open sewage ditch pungent with the smells of farm life, past a sleepy white cow, who rises to her feet in astonishment at our arrival, we come out into a clearing dimly lit by candlelight. I am frightened, although I'm not sure why. Perhaps it is because everything is dark and the country is alien. Perhaps it is because I know the dead man is waiting for us.

Crouched in the clearing, dozens of mourners stare intensely at the ground. At first, I think they must be praying over the man. Panic grips me. My heart catches in my throat and I am suddenly nauseated. I have never seen a dead body, except for one brief moment at my grandmother's funeral when I was thirteen.

As we get closer, I am astonished to see they are gambling, and all they are staring at is a pair of dice. Apparently it is customary to gamble at wakes and give part of the winnings (the *tong*) to the widow to pay for the funeral.

We continue towards the back of the property, past the chickens sleeping in the trees and the dusty stalks of recently cut sugarcane, to where there is a small nipa hut with an entry ladder made of tree limbs bound together with jute rope. Three adults and two children live in this one-room hut. I climb the ladder behind Mely and find myself inside with the deceased, his widow, and his oldest daughter.

The casket takes up one-third of the room, and it is closed, but there is a small, clear glass window over his face. Although I know he has been dead for ten days—and certainly his eyes must be shut—I imagine he is staring at us. I am horrified. I want to become very small, flatten myself against the walls of the room, and become invisible. I begin to sweat profusely, and not from the heat.

Tearing my eyes away from him, I look at his widow and daughter and observe their obvious despair. They are wearing black clothing and have torn, white rags of mourning tied around their heads. Making animal sounds born of their terrible nameless grief, they seem as if they are about to collapse. Wringing their hands and swaying ever so slightly, they speak with Mely in low tones, and I know I must leave immediately. This is too intimate, too private for a stranger to witness. What can I possibly say to these women?

Scrambling down the ladder, I make my way back to the front of the clearing and join a group of musicians, who are beginning to sing and play guitar. Sitting next to Joseph on a small, wooden bench in the deep darkness, I am overwhelmed with the impulse to lean over and smell his neck. He is completely sexy, in a way American men never are. He is brown and earthy, his muscles hardened from working in the fields.

An old man sits down on the other side of me. "I'll sing Pangasinan, because this place Pangasinan," he says, and he begins to sing a deliciously sweet song.

The children press in on us. I can feel their hot bodies and their hot breath pressing, pressing, pressing at my back. Many of them have never seen a white person before, and they devour me with their eyes. They make me nervous, and I move closer to Joseph, as if he could shield me from their gaze. They beg to touch my naked arm to see if the white color will rub off and whether underneath I am brown, like them. I ask Joseph to make the children move back, and they do, but it is so hot that even with them standing several feet behind us, I can still feel the heat of their breath on me and the hunger in their eyes.

Some of the adults begin to dance, and one very old man asks me to dance with him, but I cannot. Any movement might cause me to lose control and run away. I do not know if he will be insulted, nor at this moment do I care. Two elderly women get up and begin to dance with each other. Executing a stiff waltz, they stumble over their feet and each other, laughing hysterically. Joseph puts his arm around my waist and pulls me closer.

Everyone wants me to sing, so I play a Grateful Dead song about trying to run away from the devil—because it is quick and happy and they will not know what I am saying anyway. Joseph leans over and whispers in my ear that everyone thinks we are married. It has become a circus as well as a wake, and except for the dead man, I have become the major attraction.

Mely and the choir pass us on their way back to the jeepney. They have finished the service and the blessing of the man, who can now finally be buried. Mely looks at me with a question and a twinkle in her eyes as if she is wondering whether her guest from America has been behaving herself.

The next morning at breakfast, she says, "I'm so proud because you made the people happy with your singing. You helped them forget their sorrow."

The Miracle and the Enigma

Another belief central to the faith of the early Filipinos was the existence of a Supreme Sky God, who was invisible and sacred. This God was so far above man that lower deities existed to intercede between Him and man. They also believed in a Trinity that included the Sky God, his Son, and the invisible but all-powerful aspect of God, often depicted as an eye within a triangle sending out rays of spiritual illumination in every direction. This aspect of God became known as the *Holy Spirit* after the incorporation of Christianity. Paintings depicting this eye can be seen hanging above the altar in many present-day Spiritist churches throughout the Philippines.

Cultures around the world have different beliefs about heaven and hell, with some believing in varying levels where souls reside, depending on the manner of life and death of each individual. The early Filipinos believed there was life after death in a heaven called *Langit*, which was represented by the blue sky above them. The idea of hell did not exist in their theology until after the arrival of Christianity. They also believed in magic, earth spirits, demonic forces, and respect for the power of the natural elements.

Continued on page 71.

Joseph and Rosa

◦—◌▪◈▪◌—◦

An dai magtrabaho mayong aanihon.
He who does not work will harvest nothing.

The next day, after sitting with Joseph so intimately at the old man's wake, I am disappointed to learn that he lives with Rosa, and most likely they are married. The rest of the family seems to disapprove of Rosa, but perhaps they tolerate her because of her relationship with Joseph. He is the oldest male in the family, and he is also the Barangay Captain, an elected position that allows him some control over matters affecting the entire community. A *barangay* is the smallest unit of local government in Filipino society, consisting of 50 to 100 families, who are responsible to a Captain, who reports, in turn, to a higher governmental authority.

Rosa is always in motion. Her duties begin before dawn and last until she has prepared the evening meal and washed the dishes. Cooking is accomplished over an open fire in the clay oven just outside the door. The family also eats outside. Her chores include taking care of the pigs, laundry and ironing, and preparing rice to be fermented into vinegar. The ever-present smell of vinegar seeps out of the lidded, ceramic crocks sitting in the dirt surrounding the house of Rosa and Joseph.

They live the way farmers have lived for centuries: focused on basic survival. Rosa gathers firewood in order to cook, or she goes to town to buy charcoal when she can afford it. Her house has a small sink with running cold water, but when she needs hot water she heats it on the outdoor fire. In order to wash the family's clothes, Rosa must first carry them about a mile to a small river. She does not use Mely's pump with the other women.

After washing and drying the clothes, she builds a fire to heat her iron, which really is made of iron. I have only seen one like it once before, in a Civil War museum in Texas. Yet, despite the potential obstacles to cleanliness, Rosa's two children emerge from the house every morning immaculately dressed in their school uniforms. The teenage girl has a sour expression, as if she is angry. Jaime, her younger brother, is hyperactive. Rosa chases him through the compound several times a day, screaming his name.

Rosa frowns when I enter her house. She keeps her face hidden behind her work-worn hands, as if she believes she is unattractive or expects me to be critical. Often standing in a darkened corner rubbing her fingers repeatedly on her stained apron, she whispers to no one in particular, "I'm ashamed." She must have a deep inferiority complex, resulting in anxiety about everything, including visitors.

Rosa wants more money and a better lifestyle. However, there are few opportunities to earn money in the rural Philippines, other than selling farm products with a minimal return. Like Lucy's husband, Rosa once managed to get a permit to work overseas. She went to Singapore, where she was treated like a slave, but left just a few months short of her two-year contract. She said it was "homesick versus dollars" that made her come back to Vacante. After twenty-two months of working as a maid, she returned home with only $200 because of the penalties for not fulfilling her contract. A second attempt to get a work permit (this time for Saudi Arabia) failed, after costing her 3,000 pesos ($120) in application fees. At the time of this writing, Rosa has been working in Spain as a maid for several years and sending money home.

The Miracle
and the Enigma

In modern times, one of the foremost characteristics of the "New Age" philosophies, Neo-Paganism, shamanism, and other forms of occultism is the return to the ancient idea that the spirit world and the material world are different aspects of a greater reality, existing simultaneously, and that everything is alive and sacred. All of the ancient societies around the world had belief systems and rituals based on animism, and as new religions arose, including Buddhism, Hinduism, Islam, and Christianity, the old and new religions were merged to varying degrees.

The Philippines is the only country in East Asia that is primarily Christian: 73 percent—with 7 percent Muslim, 18 percent derived from Christianity, and 2 percent traditional religions making up the rest. Although many modern-day Filipinos make fun of the old ways, and despite the conversion of the majority of the country to Christianity, many Filipinos still carry the beliefs of their ancestors, resulting in a culture that is fond of ritual and superstition.

Continued on page 75.

Making Molasses

Matam-is kun atong tunlon, ro suhoe ko atong pamugon.
Sweet to us are the fruits of our labor.

The heat lies heavy on the land. The newly-planted sugarcane sleeping in the dry soil waits for rain, which is not expected for another month. The restless pigs make deep groaning sounds, and the oldest one chews passionately on the wooden boards restraining her. She stares up at me as I gaze out of the window of my nipa hut. The ducks, chickens, and dogs lie sleeping in the dust, later to wake when the coolness of evening descends and they become a chorus demanding dinner.

In the front yard, some visitors from a distant province are conferring with Mely. The sound of their soft voices chattering in their native language washes over me as I sit on my bed and write. Outside the window, several children are singing, dancing, and banging one another about. My favorite child, Minchu, has been playing all morning with an empty shampoo bottle she found in the trash, tossing it repeatedly in the air and squealing with joy as she catches it again. It is remarkable how little it takes to entertain her and the other children.

When I first met Minchu, her legs from the knees down were covered with open sores. Flies hovered around them. I applied calendula lotion every day for about a week, and soon the sores were completely healed. After that, the fragile child followed me everywhere, saying "Very good boy," the only English she knew, and patting me affectionately.

A rooster crows in the distance, and I can also hear the mechanical whir of the sugarcane press. The men from our farm are making molasses from the newly-cut sugarcane. Leaving the nipa hut and crossing the road, I arrive just as they are finishing a rest period and are about to begin working again.

A motorized belt fifteen feet long runs the complex set of gears that operates the press. One man pours gasoline into the engine, while three others pull hard on the belt. Once the belt begins to move, a teenage boy carries the stalks into the shed from the yard, where two others feed them into one side of the press. The juice is run off through a long pipe into the cooking pots. The crushed stalks are pushed out of the other side of the press and tied in bundles. Another worker puts the bundles on top of his head and carries them out to the sun to dry.

At one end of the long, low, and terribly hot shed, the pressed juice is cooking in pots about four feet across. Two boys feed the sun-dried stalks left from a previous pressing into the fire through small holes in the ground. Here, nothing is wasted—even the grains of rice that fall from the dishes when they are being washed are collected and thrown outside in the dirt for the chickens.

The juice is bubbling furiously in the pots and the foam rising to the top boils over and is scooped off. After an hour or so, the juice has boiled down into thick creamy molasses, a lovely shade of gold. This golden sweetness is poured into huge barrels to cool. Eventually, it will be taken to a commercial sugar factory for further processing.

A dozen or so barefoot children of different ages are playing near the shed. Four-year-old Jaime shouts with joy as he throws himself over and over again into the piles of drying sugarcane stalks. An older girl stands next to one of the barrels of cooling molasses, a dreamy faraway look in her eyes. She has one hand raised to her mouth as she sucks the delicious sweetness dripping from her fingers, while with her other hand she traces sticky designs in the top of the settling molasses.

The press runs twenty-four hours a day during harvest season. The pungent smell of the cooking molasses pervades the countryside, seeping into everything. Sometimes, the smell wakes me in the middle of the night, and I lie there thinking about how much I will miss the soft whirring sound of the press and the fragrance of molasses when I leave Pangasinan.

After planting the sugarcane, irrigating the fields, harvesting and hauling the stalks to the pressing shed, and finally thirty or more hours of back-breaking labor to produce molasses, Joseph will earn about $12 per barrel.

As I watch the men and boys working, Joseph comes and stands next to me. "Perhaps it would be easier to pick grapes in California," he says.

The Miracle
and the Enigma

Retention of some of the elements of animism has led to what is known as "Folk Catholicism." Ancient and modern belief systems exist side by side, as can be seen in the worship of patron saints (which replaces worship of ancient spirits or individual Gods) and the wearing of the cross or crucifix to ward off evil spirits. Christian shrines have been built on the same sites as former animist shrines, and may still be used for mystical or psychic purposes.

Thus, although many Filipinos visit their church on a regular basis, they may also visit a faith healer for health reasons or because of interpersonal difficulties. They might even make sacrifices to bribe the spirits for prosperity, good health, or bountiful crops. Folk Catholicism is found in both the educated and uneducated, and in rural and urban dwellers alike.

Continued on page 78.

The Carabao

Kung kalabaw ay sa lubid, kung tao ay sa bibig.
A carabao is caught by his rope, and man by his word.

I often wake at three or four in the morning when I am sleeping in the nipa hut and lie silently in bed listening to the wind whispering in the grass roof, the stirring of the dreaming dogs, the intermittent crowing of the cocks, and the ducks and chickens grouped in a circle outside my window in the moonlight. They make soft cooing sounds, and appear to be having a meeting, a discussion, or maybe they're just laying eggs.

About this time, Joseph comes out of his house—white shirt against dark skin—rubbing his sleepy eyes. He unties his carabao and leads him into the irrigation ditch for a bath. Speaking in low tones, he murmurs "duh, duh," and the massive creature lies down so Joseph can pour buckets of cool water over his hairy back. Hitching the carabao to a wooden cart with enormous wheels, Joseph leads him towards the fields, where they will cut and haul sugarcane until the mid-morning heat becomes oppressive.

The beast is large, very large, brown, and slightly hairy with enormous horns. I have tried hard to understand the docile carabao, stared longingly into his eyes seeking knowledge of who he is, seeking communion with him. But his nature is more mystical than mine, and he is beyond my reach. Sometimes in the afternoon when Joseph is sleeping in his hammock and everyone else is sitting on the porch eating sour, green mangoes spread with fresh molasses, I sense he is thirsty because of the beads of sweat rising up on his large flat nose. So, I carry a bucket of water from the irrigation ditch and offer it to him. He drinks it quickly in big slurping gulps, eyeing me suspiciously. He tolerates me only if I move slowly.

Wandering towards the river one morning, I meet Buyat, Minchu's father, who is plowing the field for the next crop of sugarcane. The smell of the overturned dirt is intoxicating, and I beg him to let me try the ancient metal plow. He hands me the curved wooden handle, worn smooth by years and perhaps centuries of use. The children, who follow me everywhere, laugh when they see me barefoot in the dirt with plow in hand and carabao standing ready. Tugging on the rope tied to his nose ring, I shout, "Duh."

This is supposed to make him move, pulling the plow, but he only turns his head around to look at me in surprise. Again I shout, "Duh," and again the same reaction. Minchu and the other children point at me and roll on the ground screaming with laughter. I look to Buyat for help. He smiles respectfully and, taking the rope from my hands, murmurs, "Duh." His deep voice rings with *quiet* authority, and the carabao responds immediately, trudging down the field with me scrambling along behind him trying to hold onto the plow and dig an acceptable furrow.

Later, when the sun is low in the sky and we are walking back to the house, Minchu gently takes my hand and looks up at me. Her face radiating love and total trust, she whispers "Thank you."

This is a simple life lived close to the land. Things happen in a concrete and sequential way that requires significantly more effort than driving to the supermarket. The farmer digs the ground, plants the seeds, waters them faithfully, harvests the crops, and then later his wife prepares dinner.

I feel peaceful in a way I have never felt before, and I want to hold onto this feeling. Perhaps I will plant potatoes when I get back to Berkeley.

The Miracle
and the Enigma

Spiritism and Spiritualism

These two terms are closely related and often confused. *Webster's Dictionary* adds to the confusion by giving them the same definition: "(1) the view that spirit is a prime element of reality; (2) a belief that spirits of the dead communicate with the living, usually through a *medium* . . . ; and (3) a religious movement."

Both Spiritism and Spiritualism have common beginnings. First, with Emanuel Swedenborg (1688–1772), who at age 56 experienced visions of the spirit world and claimed to have talked with angels, devils, and spirits by visiting heaven and hell.

Next, Franz Mesmer (1734–1815) discovered what he called *animal magnetism,* or *mesmerism.* The evolution of Mesmer's ideas and practices led James Braid to develop hypnosis in 1842.

Continued on page 83.

The Initiation

Ang atong pagtuo ni Bathala, maoy atong gabayan ngadto kaniya.
Our Faith in God is our guide back to Him.

Jesus is worshiped at the Faith in God Spiritual Church, as in all Christian churches, but the Holy Spirit is the primary focus. Depicted as an all-seeing, omnipotent, single eye within a triangle that sends out rays of light, the Holy Spirit speaks through a living person who has been trained as a medium.

Elsewhere, this might be called *channeling*, and it would probably occur at a weekend seminar with an entrance fee. But in Pangasinan, it is a matter-of-fact occurrence: every Sunday the medium gives the "message." Unfortunately, this message is spoken primarily in the native dialect, so often I do not understand what is being said. Nevertheless, I experience the intense energy that fills the church when the Holy Spirit enters the medium.

It begins with a simple song, a provocative Ilokano melody, an invitation to the Holy Spirit to make itself known to us here on Earth:

Oh Jesus, a nailangitan, nga incam awawagan. Sica apo ti mangayuan, toy adipen mo a panawam sings the choir, joined by the rest of the congregation. "Oh Jesus, make yourself known to us, come unto us, give us your counsel."

Oh Jesus, nga ubbog toy biag, Jesus nga, inanam. Sica ti mangliwliwa, ket sica apo, cadacam ti mangaywan. "Oh blessed Jesus, shower your blessings upon us, your humble servants. Through your grace we are made whole."

As usual, the singers are accompanied by an elderly musician who is banging away with great gusto on a guitar that is terribly out-of-tune. A baby somewhere in the back of the church cries out in wordless sound.

Belen approaches the front of the sanctuary accompanied by another woman, who guides and supports her as she prepares to receive the spirit. Belen braces her body against the pulpit, her eyes closed and her skin translucent. Swaying ever so slightly, she bows her head and begins to speak. Only it is not Belen who speaks, but rather the Holy Spirit who speaks through her.

While she speaks, she also scribbles with a pencil on the tablet in front of her, although she does not look at the paper while she writes. This type of *automatic writing* is one way that mediums in trance (also called *trance mediums*) receive messages from the spirit world, although Belen's writing is entirely illegible. Automatic writing is also a way to *ground* the medium and help her keep in touch with her physical body while she is in a trance.

Belen's sermon is filled with references to the Bible and admonishments to specific individuals, as well as to the congregation as a whole. I am able to understand bits and pieces of it by asking Luna to translate the more dramatic parts. Belen lets the Bible fall open at random several times, and the verses she sees first are given as the study assignment for the coming week.

"Jessie. She wants you up to the front," says Luna, jabbing me in the ribs with her elbow.

"What . . . ?"

"GO. The Holy Spirit is calling you to the front."

I rise and move forward until I am standing in front of Belen. She indicates I should hold out my hands, palms up. She begins to make a spinning motion over them with her own hands, as if to create a receptive opening.

Although I did not understand it at the time, I later learned she was opening my hand chakras in order to let the energy of the Holy Spirit flow into them.

Chakras are energy centers in the etheric body, which is the layer in the energy field surrounding the physical body that is closest to the body. Chakras are the areas of interconnection between the body and spirit, and they correspond to major nerve ganglia branching out from the spinal column. Many people believe there are seven chakras; some think there are more.

Next Belen makes downward motions, as if she is pouring something into the centers of my palms. Finally, she firmly closes my hands together in prayer fashion and delicately traces the outline of each of my fingers with hers. It feels like she is sealing in what has been left there in order to protect it.

"You have received the power of Jesus Christ to do healing. When you see a man . . . and he has a pain in his head . . . touch his head . . . and he will be well."

She delivers this dramatic statement in a slow, deliberate manner. She does not open her eyes as she speaks.

Picking up the Bible, she again allows it to fall open at random. Pointing to a particular passage, she tells the church secretary to write it down and give it to me. On the paper is written "5 The Acts 17-25."

Later, when I look up this particular verse, I find that it talks about several of the Apostles, who were put into prison: "But the angel of the Lord by night opened the prison doors and brought them forth, and said: 'Go, stand and speak in the temple to the people all the words of this life'." Thus were they released from prison and went to teach the people.

I can relate to this verse, because I often feel like I am in prison—the prison of my own negativity and delusion that I am separate from God. But I hope this doesn't mean I'll have to start giving sermons. I wouldn't know how to begin or what to say.

On the way back to my seat, I pause in front of Mely and ask her what Belen meant.

"When you are given the gift of healing, the Holy Spirit also gives you a simple assignment. For me, it was to work with the long muscles of the body. Begin healing and your ability will grow."

Mely's words are incomprehensible. I am the flawed girl, the rejected girl, the one who needs help. How could I possibly heal anyone else?

Back in my seat next to Luna, I sit stunned. Joseph causes further confusion by leaning over and whispering in my ear, "I knew it. I knew it would be you."

The woman who has been standing behind Belen begins to rub Belen's arms and shoulders vigorously, presumably to bring her back into her body. As she begins to regain normal consciousness, Belen slumps over slightly and is helped back to her chair.

After the final hymn, several of us give *magnetic healing* to those in need. This is a way of removing negative energy, while also channeling positive energy into a person. It is difficult to concentrate because there is so much going on around me. Basically, the person receiving healing stands in the center of the circle of healers, who direct their open palms toward the person. This allows the energy of the Holy Spirit to flow through them and into the "patient."

"You give the *spiritual injection*," says Belen, who is almost her normal self again. Instantly, an even stronger current of energy begins to flow into the top of my head and down through my body, exploding out of the end of my pointed index finger and into the person standing in front of me. It is very much like giving an actual injection. The flow of energy feels incredibly good, and I would like spend more time with each person in order to explore this new experience, but there are too many of them, and they move quickly in and out of the circle.

Later that evening, several of us visit a woman who is suffering from high blood pressure and nervousness. Huge clouds of mosquitoes rise and encircle us as we walk down the dark, muddy road to her nipa hut. After ascending a bamboo ladder, we sit quietly, illuminated only by the light of a kerosene lantern. The choir sings while Mely consults with the woman. Then we form a circle and give her magnetic healing. Belen and I massage her back, which is muscle-bound and tense from farm work.

Afterwards, we laugh and talk, and the woman seems content. Our love and caring is the true medicine. This is how life should be lived: in a community that first nurtures itself, and then radiates love out in ever-widening circles until the possibility exists for everyone in the world to be at peace and filled with joy.

The Miracle
and the Enigma

In 1848, the Fox sisters played an important role in the creation of Spiritualism. They began to hear curious rapping sounds coming from their basement, which led to channeling sessions in an attempt to make contact with the spirit that was creating the sounds. They claimed they were able to communicate with a peddler who had been killed and buried beneath their house. They became quite famous as a result.

Although the claims made by the Fox sisters later proved to be false, the belief in the ability to communicate with the dead continued to grow, becoming a religious movement that was given the name *Spiritualism*.

Continued on page 86.

Auntie Buyat

Masapulan ti asawa ngem saan, ti ina.
One can look for a mate but not for a mother.

She carries with her the musty smell of cigars, fish, and mothballs. One lone tooth juts out from the front of her mouth, and she is dressed as if someone went to a secondhand store and randomly picked out her wardrobe. The only name I know her by is *Auntie*, the name given to all of the adult women—except when they are called *Mother* by their own children. She is the mother of Buyat, so I call her *Auntie Buyat*.

She cannot speak a word of English, nor I her language, but she speaks to me with her eyes, deep brown and with a twinkle that it makes it seem as if she is always laughing at some great cosmic joke. Most of all she speaks to me with her incredibly strong hands: gnarled knuckles, soft palms, freckled skin. These are hands that have ploughed the fields, prepared food, pounded laundry on the river rocks, made love, birthed babies, and comforted children. Always, they have soothed and caressed without question.

But for tonight, and the other nights that will follow, her hands belong to me because she is my *mangngilut* (manual therapist). I give her 25 pesos and a small packet of her favorite cigars each time we meet.

Her face is round and freckled like her hands, and it is very large, much too large for her tiny body. She appears to be shrinking, except for her face. I do not know her actual age, but she must be at least eighty. She lives with Buyat and his family. During the day, she sweeps the fallen leaves in front of their nipa hut, but at night she makes her way across the narrow log spanning the irrigation ditch, holding the rope handrail with one hand and her wooden cane with the other. The children scamper back and forth over this log, but watching Auntie Buyat cover the same distance is disconcerting. She is both graceful and awkward, as she tap, tap, taps her cane on the log for balance. I watch from my window and hope she does not fall.

She makes her way up the polished bamboo stairs, enters my room, and greets me with a firm embrace, during which she buries her face in the crook of my neck and takes a long, slow smell of me—she does this every time we meet, no matter where we are or who is watching (this is called *ungngo,* and is similar to a kiss). She usually admires my American-made matches and shyly indicates she wants some for her cigars. Sometimes she asks me to rub lotion on her arthritic knees.

Auntie Buyat speaks to me in a steady stream of Pangasinanese while we are together, and although I do not consciously understand her, I believe our communication goes beyond verbal language. I smile and periodically mumble "Yes," although I do not *really* know what we are talking about. She, in turn, does not seem confused when I speak to her in English. Perhaps she is senile.

Pulling the mosquito net back from above the bed, I lie down on my stomach and she begins to rub my back with mentholated oil. Her touch is steady and sure, but she is also as tender as a mother. She gives special attention to my injured shoulder, which has bothered me for several years. Her therapy grows deeper and more insistent each night we are together, until eventually my shoulder no longer hurts.

I fall into a deep sleep when she leaves, the faint aroma of wintergreen lingering on my skin.

The Miracle
and the Enigma

News of the Fox sisters reached France, catching the interest of Allan Kardec, whose birth name was Léon-Dénizarth-Hippolyte Rival. Kardec's interest in what he would later call *Spiritism* began with the use of *talking boards* to communicate with the dead. Talking boards were an early version of the Ouija boards that later became quite popular.

Kardec published his first book in 1857: *The Spirit's Book*, which included a series of questions posed by Kardec to spirits channeled through two mediums and the responses of the spirits. These channeled entities claimed that they spoke to Kardec because he had an important religious mission to fulfill. He also defined his work in this book, calling it the *Spiritist Doctrine*. He went on to write three more books, including: *The Book of Mediums, The Gospel as Interpreted by Spiritism,* and *Spiritualist Initiation.* (10)

Continued on page 90.

The Filipino Elvis Presley

Ti arac managrabrabac.
Wine creates a jovial atmosphere.

Since early morning, the man known locally as the "Filipino Elvis Presley" has been carefully stirring the contents of a large pot over an open fire on the other side of the irrigation ditch. He was given this nickname because of the emotion that pours from his slight, angular frame when he sings—as if every cell of his body is lamenting his own, private "Heartbreak Hotel." Although he is blind in one eye and has a large gap in the front of his mouth where he is missing two teeth, he is quite attractive.

I am distracted from thinking about Elvis when visitors arrive. Descending from several jeepneys parked in front of the church, they are dressed in their Sunday clothes, the children scrubbed until their faces shine. The adults are carrying packages and bedrolls bound with twine.

"Today we welcome our Brothers and Sisters from Maria Aurora," announces Mely. "They have traveled many hours to celebrate The Lord with us."

Soon everyone is drifting to the patio behind the church, and the packages are piled on a table. The visiting women, who are wearing nylon stockings even in the stifling heat, sit and begin to fan themselves. They look like a bouquet of drooping flowers. Mely welcomes each person individually and, as usual, I do not understand most of the conversation. They are from an isolated, mountain province far to the east and do not speak English. I can only observe as Mely and Trinidad serve the guests tall glasses of sweet, lukewarm tea and cookies. After awhile, the women retire to the house to begin cooking, and the children disappear in the direction of the basketball court.

My gaze begins to wander again across the irrigation ditch. Most of the men have gathered in front of Buyat's nipa hut. They are sitting in a large circle, laughing and singing, and they appear to be passing a bottle around.

Drawn to their laughter, and to Elvis and his pot, I balance myself carefully on the log that crosses the ditch, inching my way slowly. When I arrive at the circle of men, at first they seem disconcerted by my presence. Perhaps a Filipino woman would never be so bold as to join in the camaraderie of men.

But then Joseph smiles. "Jessica, sit here with us," he says, motioning to a chair beside him. "I will give you a taste of *basi*, sugarcane wine."

This produces some snickering among the assembled men—perhaps they are aware of the attraction between Joseph and me. They watch closely as he pours some of the clear liquid into a small glass, their joking silenced. Taking a sip, I begin to choke violently. Gasping for breath, I nearly fall on the ground. Basi is strong like vodka or tequila, but my "initiation" must be completed. I drink the rest of the wine quickly and without further difficulty. The men applaud and roar their approval.

They return to their drinking and gossiping, and my attention is drawn back to Elvis, who is a short distance away, still stirring. Unnoticed by the others, I quietly approach him.

"What are you cooking in your pot?"

"Ah, Jes-se-ka, this is *very* special. This soup is the head of the dog. It makes man very strong with woman."

He says this with great reverence, as I gasp and recoil backwards from him and the pot, my American love of pets standing in stark contradiction to the Filipino habit of eating just about anything. Consider *balut*, for example: fertilized eggs containing the partially-formed bodies of ducks, which are boiled and eaten. (Balut are also believed to have aphrodisiac qualities.)

Unable to come to terms with either the idea of eating the family dog or the mystery of male virility, I decide it would be better to return to the more reasonable activity of cooking with the other women.

Late in the afternoon, when a feast has been spread out on long tables, everyone gathers together again for food and conversation. Soon night comes, and Elvis and the other musicians begin to make music. Everyone starts dancing: women with women, old with young. There are no social reservations in this large, extended family of "brothers and sisters," where each individual is loved and respected equally.

Satiated with dinner, consisting mostly of *lumpia* (Filipino egg rolls) and *pancit* (fried noodles), I leave and wander towards the basketball court, where some of the men have begun to play ball. Many of them are still drinking, and they are all smoking cigarettes "to keep the mosquitos away."

Joseph picks up my guitar and begins to sing "Lovers' Moon," a song about two lovers who are a world apart. As he sings, I wonder whether the song will be about us in some not-too-distant future:

"There's a lovers' moon tonight, shining down
    on half of this world.
So many souls are in its light, but for me there is just one soul . . .
Waiting, I know she's waiting;
I know she waits for me under the lovers' moon."

Glancing over my shoulder, I notice Luna standing behind me. She has the face of an angel. My breath catches in my throat because I have never seen anything so beautiful. She moves towards me and wraps herself around my back for warmth because it has become chilly. We sit together in perfect contentment and watch the players. They are moving shadows illuminated by moonlight filtered through a fine, ethereal mist. The tap, tap, tap of the ball as it hits the cement, the squeaking of shoes, and Luna's soft breath in my ear are the only sounds to be heard, and it occurs to me: *Nothing* needs to be any different than it already is.

The Miracle
and the Enigma

The differences between Spiritualism and Spiritism are best described by Heather Cumming in her book about "John of God," a psychic surgeon and spiritual healer from Brazil, who has treated millions of people over the past forty years:

"Spiritualism and Spiritism both share the belief that communication with the deceased is possible. The spirits are contacted through mediums, who communicate directly with these spirits to bring through messages, guidance, support, and healing. Spiritualism does not follow a particular doctrine, whereas Spiritism is a collection of tenets and lessons taken directly from highly evolved spirits such as Jesus. These teachings comprise the philosophy and practice of Spiritism."(11) (See also (12) and (13) for more information about John of God.)

Continued on page 93.

Rosita Agaid

Elek kay susto, pian naentang kad sakit na ulo.
Laugh loud so your headache may be relieved.

After church in Vacante and a quick lunch, I catch a tricycle to Binalonan, and then a jeepney to the church of Rosita Agaid in Tarlac, a village about twenty miles away. It is crowded and unbearably hot by the time I arrive, but fortunately the woman in charge moves me to the top of the long list because she knows the heat is hard on foreigners. Many of the people in the waiting crowd begin to giggle when they see me sitting in the front row.

I have brought Rosita a gift: a box of business cards with gold-embossed lettering. The gold on the cards and the gold of her earrings match the gold she carries in one of her front teeth, which flashes brightly with her constant laughter.

There are babies and small children who cry in their mothers' arms, and old people who sit silent and stoic. The ailments are varied and many. I take my place in the crowd that leans forward with great anticipation to watch the small table at the front of the room. Most of the Filipino Spiritualist Churches have a closed-door healing room that each person enters alone, but at Rosita's everything is out in the open; it is almost theatrical. The table is surrounded by several female assistants, who hold up sheets so no one will be embarrassed by being seen partially naked in public.

My turn comes quickly. After getting on the table, while also trying to keep my underwear from public view, I look up into the golden face of Rosita smiling down at me.

First she puts her hand between my legs (but not inside of me) and gives a tremendous shove, causing me to scream loudly. *This is certainly not what I expected.* All of the women standing around the table begin roaring with laughter. Even Rosita looks surprised.

"WHAT was that?" I ask.

"Womb moved to proper place," she answers.

Next she moves aside my clothing and begins to knead my stomach. Suddenly, the whole scene seems far away, as if I am watching it from somewhere else. I am floating, at peace.

∘∘◁▷✳◁▷∘∘

Rosita Agaid is gone now—passed on to where we will all go one day. But I remember her gold-framed tooth and how it sparkled when she laughed her wide and generous smile. And how she winked at me when she put her hand up under my skirt, with certainty, as if the knowledge of all womankind was there in her hand. She leaned against the edge of the table to brace herself until she found the center of the universe within, the center of healing.

Then she lightly laid her hands on me and the entire universe exploded into a million bright stars, showering down blessings that filled us and the entire room. And afterwards, everyone was laughing—I was laughing—and her gold tooth, how it sparkled, how it shone.

The Miracle
and the Enigma

Both Spiritualism and Spiritism employ a technic known as *automatic writing*, which involves writing that does not come from the conscious thoughts of the writer. It is a way for trance mediums, and sometimes ordinary people, to receive communications from the spirit world. The writer's hand forms the message, but they are unaware of what is being written. One of the most interesting automatic writers was Helene Smith, an early 20th century psychic who felt that her automatic writing was the attempt of Martians to communicate with people on Earth. She claimed she could translate their Martian language into French. (14)

Kardec's Spiritist Doctrine began to spread throughout the world, and had a profound influence on the Filipino Christian Spiritists, who saw in his teachings confirmation of their own beliefs about spiritual reality. The Spiritists of the Philippines had long been ignored or persecuted outright, but in Allan Kardec's teachings they found vindication. His Spiritist Doctrine provided an unprecedented explanation of the nature of the spirit world and the role of the Holy Spirit. Harvey Martin has written a fascinating book that discusses Spiritism in the Philippines; *The Secret Teachings of the Espiritistas.* (15)

Continued on page 97.

David Oligane Speaks to a Witch

An macacadacop nin aswang, ang capariho aswang.
A witch can be caught only by another witch.

David Oligane's chapel is one of the many small healing centers scattered throughout Pangasinan. Located about ten miles east of Urdaneta in a quiet farming community, the chapel is visited by both locals and groups of foreigners. Luna and I make the trip in a hired tricycle. Passing through the bucolic countryside, the teenage tricycle driver swerves around wagons drawn by carabao and large patches of rice laid out on the roads to dry in the sun.

When we arrive, David's wife, Mary, leads us into the combination chapel and healing room. An enormous painting takes up one entire wall. At the top of the painting are the Latin words: *Aveminus Triumphasis*, which loosely translated means: "Hail the Triumph [of the Holy Spirit]."

The primary object in the painting is a large, blue eye. It is a bit frightening. Light streams from the eye and is transposed lightly over the entire picture. Below the eye is a white dove sitting atop a globe representing the Earth. Unfortunately, before the artist created the painting, the sheetrock was not primed and the nails were not covered with plaster. Consequently, there are uniform rows of rust marks bleeding through to the surface, marring the design.

We introduce ourselves, and when David hears I am from the U.S., he says, "I had a vision of California and Japan. Volcanoes will explode and the whole West Coast of America will become a string of islands. This message is from Spirit. I think it will happen after the year 2000."

While we are talking, David watches me with a vacant, yet focused expression. He seems to have fallen into a trance similar to that of the other healers and mediums I have met. Trapped like a firefly in a covered jar, I flutter nervously as he evaluates my health and sincerity.

Gently taking my hands, he blows on them and tells me where the pain in my body is located. Then, kneeling in front of me, he pinches my left toe, causing a sharp needle-like pain that lasts about twenty seconds. As he presses, he exclaims loudly, "Hello, Hello."

Mary tells us David is talking to the witch who has inhabited my body and is causing my illness. Each healer is said to have specific abilities, and David Oligane is believed to be a witch hunter and exorcist.

He instructs me to lie down on a low table and expose my stomach. Then he kneads my flesh until he finds the problem area. Holding one of his index fingers about two inches above my body he makes a jerking motion. I feel a strong current of energy coming from his finger, and a two-inch, bloody scratch appears, even though he has not actually touched me.

Grabbing a small glass, he presses it to my skin over the scratch and applies heat to the end of the glass with burning cotton. After about a minute, he removes the glass and his hand enters my abdomen. Pulling out crumbled pieces of what appears to be white, fatty tissue, he drops them into a glass of water. This treatment is rather uncomfortable, but fortunately it is followed by massage.

"How do you feel?" he asks.

"Light, expanded, very relaxed."

<hr />

Next, David performs the same procedure on Luna, focusing primarily on her back. This time he asks *me* to hold *my* finger above her skin in order to make the scratch. As he moves my hand with his, a scratch appears beneath my pointed index finger, even though I have not touched Luna's skin.

He applies the glass with heat to Luna's back as he did with me, but he does not remove any tissue. Luna is young and must not have any significant health problems.

"How much should we give for healing?" I ask him, as we prepare to leave.

"From the heart only," he replies.

So, I give him $20. As we drive away, I look back and see him standing in the doorway of the chapel with his arm around Mary's waist. They are both smiling.

The Miracle
and the Enigma

The melding of Christianity, Spiritist theology, and traditional Filipino beliefs culminated in the founding of the *Union Espiritista Christiana de Filipinas* (the "Union") in the Philippines on February 19, 1905. According to Harvey Martin:

"Members of the Union believed the Holy Spirit to be the *Divine Minister* and guide, sent to them by Jesus to illuminate the mysteries of the Bible and to help them establish the kingdom of heaven on earth. The study of the scriptures under the tutelage of the Holy Spirit was high on the agenda of the Union members, as was the ministry of healing." (15)

Continued on page 104.

Mission to Maria Aurora

◦—◧✳◧—◦

An kagadanan sa kamot nin Diyos.
Death is in God's hands.

Lying motionless on the cement floor of the church with only a thin blanket beneath me, I stare at the ceiling, the crepe paper flowers hanging above me silent, unmoving. I feel paralyzed. My entire body hurts. Even the effort to breathe makes me dizzy. I have food poisoning from eating chicken at the open market in Urdaneta.

Too weak to move, I begin to pray for something to ease my misery. Soon Trinidad arrives, but the sound of her voice is irritating. All I can do is moan. I want Joseph. Pressing my body deeper into the coolness of the floor, I whisper, "Joseph, Joseph."

Trinidad goes to get him, and he arrives quickly. But Rosa is with him. Empowered by sickness, I wave her away like an annoying mosquito. She hesitates at first, not wanting to leave me alone with him, but then she realizes I am too sick to seduce anybody, and certainly not in the church. After she leaves, Joseph sits with me and holds my hand until evening, when my fever drops and I am able to return to my room. The next day I am feeling better, but still weak.

A few days later, a letter arrives via tricycle messenger. After reading it, Mely turns to me and says, "Jessica, we go to mission. Our church in Maria Aurora has invited us."

We leave in the jeepney before dawn the next day—Rosa does not go with us. Joseph drives east, first crossing the wide flood plain that runs north/south through the center of Luzon. This area is an enormous river when it rains, but now, in the dry season, the jeepney raises a cloud of dust. Mile after mile, the wind flows through the open windows bringing with it the smell of the dry fields, cow manure, cooking fires, and molasses. The dust of the road contains everything that has ever existed. This fine powder, carried around the world by breeze, squall, and tempest, might once have been my ancestor, the clouds of another planet, or even my own body. When Joseph stops the jeepney for a short break, I wander out into the fields, my sandaled feet kicking up some farmer's forgotten furrow, and I feel as if I am touching the stars, the moon, the very heart of God. I meet myself in the fragmented earth.

Continuing on, the rough, winding road begins to rise, higher and higher into the Sierra Madre Mountains of Aurora Province. This undeveloped area is the birthplace of Manuel Quezon, a politician who led the struggle for independence and became the first President of the Philippine Commonwealth in 1935; *Aurora Province* is named for his wife. After steep mountains, the land slopes back down and becomes a wild coast with high cliffs. The surfing scene in Francis Ford Coppola's *Apocalypse Now* was filmed on the beaches below.

After the intense heat of the lowlands, I am grateful for the greenery and cool air of the mountains. We arrive in the village of Maria Aurora just as the sun is going down. Descending from the jeepney, we are welcomed by a crowd of about twenty-five villagers.

"My brothers and sisters from Faith in God, we welcome you to our humble church," says one of the older women, her open arms outstretched towards us.

It is indeed humble, not much more than a simple hut made from bamboo slats and with a dirt floor. Inside, a potted plant with bright red flowers and a framed painting similar to the one on David Oligane's chapel wall are the only decorations. There is a plain, wooden table in front of the painting. The rest of the room is filled with benches.

The service begins almost immediately. For me, it is long and dreary, involving hours of preaching and hymn singing. The purpose of this intense, focused activity is to call forth the Divine Energy of the Holy Spirit in preparation for the healing session in the morning.

But I am hungry, having eaten little for several days, and I am so exhausted I can hardly keep my eyes open. Mely insists I entertain the congregation, but I am too weak to sing. Finally, around midnight, I realize they intend to have church until morning. When no one is looking, I slip out into the darkness. While wandering around in a daze, I come upon a large tree and fall asleep beneath it, covered only by a thin cotton jacket.

After what seems like just a few minutes, I am awakened by a man shaking my shoulder. He leads me to a small hut with a cot and a blanket. I lie down and fall asleep again, but not for long. A rooster begins to crow, and it seems like he is right next to my head. *Have they put me to bed in a chicken coop?* For several hours, I drift in and out of sleep, each time to be awakened by the screeching of the bird.

Upon leaving the hut the next morning, I am surprised to see an equally unhappy rooster on the other side of the thin, grass wall, just inches from where I had been sleeping. The frustrated creature is bound to a stake by a rope and metal loop around its ankle, perhaps to keep it from chasing the hens.

After sandwiches and thick, hot coffee for breakfast, the healing session begins. Joseph plays hymns on the guitar and everyone sings. Mely is at the front of the room wearing her blue-flowered dress with lace trim. She leans over each person, who is in full view as she works. The crowd around her seems mesmerized. She seems mesmerized. Once again, to my amazement, the miracle of psychic surgery happens right in front of me. The experience is always the same: I am totally in the "Now." I see the body opened, the blood, and the removed and discarded tissue as if for the first time. I can hardly believe my eyes. Even now, looking back, I wonder: *Did it really happen? Was it all a dream?*

Several hours later, when Mely is finished, we pile back into the jeepney and head for another village about fifty miles away, the second stop on our mission. Everyone is exhausted, and soon after arriving we are taken into the church to rest.

<hr />

Later, we sit on small wooden stools at a rectangular table in a room dimly lit by two kerosene lamps. The table is heavily laden with many different cooked foods, although it is difficult to tell what they are. Mely whispers that the family is quite poor, but they have put their resources together in order to prepare this "feast" for me, the rare and important visitor from America. She whispers that I am to taste each dish and compliment the cook, who is sitting at the head of the table watching carefully for my reaction.

I am neurotic about food. I need to know exactly what I am eating, and I definitely never eat food that is slimy. Unfortunately, everything on the table looks slimy. I begin to take small portions from each of the serving bowls as they are passed around. Soon there is the clink of forks on plates as everyone begins to eat.

Conscious of the softly murmured conversation of my fellow diners, I put the first, tiny bite to my lips. *Doesn't smell so bad; might be chicken or goat meat mixed with tomatoes and okra; I'll try closing my eyes and maybe I won't notice the depressing color and strange texture. Okay, made it through that mouthful, now try another.*

By proceeding slowly in this manner, I am able to take a small taste of each item, turn to the cook, and murmur "um," indicating the food is delicious. She is smiling; they are all smiling, and it seems I have managed to rise above an awkward situation. Only the children, who stand in the doorway pointing at me and giggling, seem to realize something is amiss—or maybe they are laughing because they have never seen a white person before and to them I look strange.

The familiar smell of rice and the hiss of the kerosene lamps are comforting, as is the fact that I have tasted the food and nothing terrible has happened. As I begin to relax into the ordinary experience of sharing a meal, I notice something drift slowly downward through the air and onto my plate. Taking my fork and tapping it lightly, I am horrified to see it move. It is a small, flying cockroach. Then another one falls dreamily from the ceiling and onto the table. Soon there are dozens of them, and I must repress a strong urge to throw up. Everyone else is still talking and eating as if nothing out-of-the-ordinary is happening.

Suddenly, I am six years old and my mother is forcing me to eat frozen peas, possibly the most disgusting thing ever created. Oh, the cruelty of parents who force small children to eat everything on their plates. But I fooled her by secreting the offensive peas under the table and depositing them on a wooden ledge, where they dried out over many years until they were unrecognizable.

But I am no longer six, nor am I clever enough to devise a way out of my current situation. Feigning calmness, I push each insect gently aside, one by one, and continue taking small bites until the meal is over and I am released from the table.

◦◦◁▷▧◁▷◦◦

The church in this village is one room, about 12 by 14 feet, and like the last place we visited, it is also made of bamboo slats with woven nipa grass for a roof. The entire front of the structure is covered with green ivy. A sign saying "Faith in God" hangs above the door-less doorway.

Inside there is the same type of painting as seen yesterday, this one covered with protective plastic sheeting. There are also benches, a blackboard, and a small table; perhaps the building is also the village school. The table has a sign attached to it saying: "Donated by Bro. and Sis. Maximo Partible."

We gather in the church after dinner, but before the regular service there is entertainment. First, "Cloud Nine" plays the harmonica, backed up by Joseph on guitar. Filipinos are fond of nicknames, and since his real name is "Claudio," he is known as "Cloud Nine," a popular candy bar.

Then it is my turn. Standing at the front of the room with my guitar, I look out over the multitude of joyful, curious faces. The large crowd extends out the door. There must be at least seventy-five adults and children in the tiny church, and more outside listening.

Joseph sits in the front row between Mely and Luna, wearing his "I Love New York" tee-shirt and casually holding a tambourine. The heat has caused a light sheen of sweat to appear on his arms and face. Without warning, my heart begins to pound, and I am filled with wild emotion as I imagine kissing his soft brown lips.

Luna's hair is tossed to one side, as she tilts her head and flashes me a radiant smile. Mely is pale and seems tired. I am momentarily taken aback, because there is so much excitement and sweetness in the room.

"I love you," I say to the entire room full of people. "I want to take your picture because you're so beautiful." Putting down the guitar, I pick up my camera and snap the photograph. Then I lead them in singing "Someone's in the Kitchen with Dina" and "Ol' MacDonald" for the children, and "Amazing Grace" for the adults.

After a short sermon and invocation, Mely performs healing on about forty people, leaning on the table for a moment between each person to conserve her strength.

As we prepare to leave the next morning, a man and a woman holding a small bundle approach Mely and me. After unwrapping part of the cloth covering, the woman holds out the bundle. Silent tears stream down her face. Inside is a grayish-blue baby, newborn and barely breathing. She wants me to hold her dying child. She expects me to perform a miracle.

Overwhelmed with compassion and other emotions I cannot even identify, I stare at the silent infant, knowing there is nothing I can do to save it. When I look deeply into the mother's sorrowful brown eyes and say, "I'm sorry," she turns to Mely with the same unspoken plea.

When faced with the stark evidence of human helplessness, nothing more can be said. No action can be taken. We can only surrender our suffering to God, because ultimately life, death, and healing belong in the realm of the Divine. Sometimes even the strength of our faith and the vast abilities of the Filipino psychic surgeons cannot alter the course of a person's fate, not even the fate of a baby.

The Miracle and the Enigma

The ARTICLES OF FAITH of the Philippines Spiritists are given in *Faith Healing and Psychic Surgery in the Philippines* (6), where the authors quote from *A Brief Doctrine of Spiritism* by J. Obdel Alexis (Juan Alvear).

Juan Alvear was a native of San Fabian, and was one of the founders of the *Union.* He was highly educated, articulate, and also the first Governor of Pangasinan. Alvear was responsible for writing a mystical history of the Espiritistas, *Antikey A Doctrina Espiritista* (A Short Spiritist Doctrine). He read Allan Kardec and studied the animistic history of the Philippines. Alvear was also a gifted healer and had a deep interest in theosophy and theology.

The ARTICLES OF FAITH were gathered by Alvear from his study of the truths of Spiritism and the writings of the "Great Apostle of Spiritism [Kardec]."

Continued on page 108.

Beach Party

Ang hudyaka ug kataw, sa pundok maoy mayong templa.
Joy and laughter are the spice of gatherings.

The fragrant smell of rice fills the house. Trinidad has been cooking since early morning, and the food is carefully packed in large baskets that fill the kitchen counters.

"We go to the beach for a picnic if you buy gasoline for the jeepney," says Mely.

Who could resist? The news spreads quickly, and children come running from every corner of the property carrying bathing suits and towels, beach hats and balls, suntan lotion, sunglasses, and musical instruments. Soon the jeepney is filled with noisy, excited children and adults.

"Jojo, the husband of Belen, would like you to drive."

Mely's voice is loud so everyone can hear, and the response is muffled laughter from behind politely-covered mouths. *She must be kidding. With only one vehicle to serve six families, why would they trust me to drive it?*

The leather driver's seat is well-worn and torn in places, and the stick shift protrudes from the floor at an odd angle. I have only driven a large truck once before, and that was twenty years ago in Los Angeles. Turning the key in the ignition, I ease up on the clutch while simultaneously pressing down on the gas. Taking the shift stick and jamming it up and left into first gear, I grab the steering wheel and hang on as the jeepney lurches out of the driveway and onto the gravel road.

The poor condition of the road and my inexperience are not the worst problems, but rather that when I hold the steering wheel steady in the middle, the front wheels do not follow. In order to keep the vehicle in the center of the road and headed in a straight direction, it is necessary to jerk the steering wheel quickly back and forth from left to right because there is about a foot and a half of "play" in the steering mechanism.

At first, the passengers think this is very funny, but their laughter turns to screaming when they realize we might crash. Joseph has taken the precautionary measure of sitting next to me so he can intervene, if necessary. I have only driven about the distance of one city block, when he grabs my shoulder and yells, "BRAKE. BRAKE. HIT THE BRAKE." Fortunately, I am able to find the pedal and we abruptly jerk to a full stop. There is a communal sigh of relief, and soon we are on our way again with Joseph behind the wheel.

The next day, I find Jojo on his back under the jeepney.

"Can you fix the steering? It's dangerous."

"I have repaired the gear box many times already. It cannot be fixed anymore, and we do not have money to buy a new one."

Further discussion reveals that even spark plugs are recycled in the Philippines by repeated cleaning, sometimes ten times or more, rather than being replaced.

<hr>

Our intended destination is San Fabian on the Gulf of Lingayen, the same beach I visited when I first arrived in Pangasinan. The forty-mile trip takes several hours because the road is under construction.

Mely has rented a nipa hut adjacent to the beach for the afternoon—not much more than a roof with four walls and sand for a floor. There is also a raised bamboo platform to sit on. The children shout with joy and race for the water, the salty tang of the sea rushing up to meet them. The rest of us stay behind to eat lunch: delicious chicken lumpia, fresh tomatoes and papaya, rice, and coffee from a thermos.

After eating, most of the adult women, especially those who are still single, refuse to come out of the nipa hut. Luna informs me she never goes out until after 4:00 P.M. because she does not want the sun to make her skin darker—evidentially, the lighter the skin color, the more desirable the female. I find this ironic. In some countries, white-skinned women go to tanning salons, while in the countries where dark skin is common the women avoid the sun, often going so far as to put white powder on their faces.

While waiting for the sun to go down, Luna starts singing:

"Tiny bubbles . . . in the wine." She takes two tiny steps to the right, swaying her hips like someone doing the hula. With the third step, she raises her arms and makes a waving movement that resembles hanging laundry on a clothesline. Then she moves back to the left as she sings, "Make me feel happy . . . make me feel fine."

"Tiny bubbles . . . make me warm all over," step right and hang laundry. "With a feeling that I'm gonna love you till the end of time," step left and repeat until you laugh so hard you almost fall over.

Soon everyone is singing and doing the improvised hula. Joseph and Buyat play guitar and bongos. It is one of the funniest things I have ever seen. When the dance changes to rock and roll, I dance with Mely, and then she dances with Trinidad, who is wearing a big floppy hat to protect her skin from the sun. We are one happy, moving entity. How could anyone ever feel lonely in a family such as this? Satiated and covered with sand, we arrive home about midnight.

The Miracle
and the Enigma

The Articles of Faith (6)

1. There is only one GOD, Creator of Heaven and Earth, of all things visible and invisible. God is eternal, without beginning and without end.
2. Man has a spirit, or soul.
3. Spirits do not die.
4. There is reincarnation, or the repeated return of the spirit to Earth to be reborn in a physical body.
5. There is a plurality of worlds.
6. There exists an eternal, continuous and endless progress or spiritual evolution of the soul. This can be attained only by obedience to God's laws and precepts of the law.
7. He who keeps the laws of God receives the corresponding reward; and he who does not keep the laws but transgresses them gets the proper and legitimate reactions or karma.
8. Spirits are felt, heard, and seen, and men on Earth can communicate with them.
9. Everybody is equal to everybody else; there is no such thing as privilege for the chosen in earthly life.
10. Without charity there is no salvation.

The National Spiritualist Association of Churches has a similar list of beliefs, called the *Declaration of Principles, Interpretation, and Definitions.* (16)

Continued on page 114.

Ramon and the Mountain City

—◦═◆═◦—

Langon a di lumenek, tatap bon makasalak.
If you keep on searching, you'll find what you are looking for.

Boarding the *Philippine Rabbit* bus stopped on the MacArthur Highway at Binalonan to pick up passengers, I am immediately assaulted by the violent drama blaring from the 13-inch television hanging above the front window. "Baguio City," I tell the driver, handing him the required fare. Taking a seat as far back as possible, I take a deep breath and relax as the bus heads north towards the mountains of Benguet Province, the air-conditioning a welcome relief after nearly a month in the lowlands.

Outside the window there are people walking along the tree-lined roadside, most of them women carrying shopping bags, each followed by several children. I am surprised to see men urinating openly. Turning away from the passing traffic, they just unzip and go, some casually looking back over their shoulders with blank stares on their faces.

Public bathrooms in the Philippines can be hard to find. The hotels have regular flush toilets, although sometimes the water pressure is low and the paper is coarse. Department stores and restaurants in Manila, bus stations, and other public facilities also have flush toilets, but the paper must be purchased for a few pesos from a woman sitting at the entrance.

Rural toilets are often a squat latrine consisting of a simple hole in the ground, five inches across, surrounded by a cement ring that slopes downward towards the hole. Travelers are expected to carry their own toilet paper or risk going without, and there is usually a faucet sticking out of the ground or a plastic bucket filled with water and a dipper for handwashing. This type of toilet is usually located in a nipa hut.

As we begin to climb higher and higher into the craggy mountains, I am jarred from my musings on comfort room facilities when the bus abruptly pulls over and comes to a halt. It's a toilet stop—a "squat and go" with no paper. Food vendors swarm around us, seemingly out of nowhere, selling soft drinks in recyclable glass bottles, peanut brittle, bucayo (coconut candy), and something oily that looks vaguely like fried pig skin.

Soon we are back on the bus and moving again. The northern Philippines experienced a major earthquake in 1990 that left large boulders protruding into the roadway, causing one-way traffic in places. The right side of the road drops away into a wild jungle abyss that is made all the more frightening by the swaying of the bus as the driver negotiates the tight curves, forcing me to turn away from the window.

Baguio in Benguet Province is a modern, Western-style city with a population of about 225,000. It is a central hub for tourists, students, and the native people, the *Igorots*, who live in the surrounding mountains and bring their produce and handicrafts to the Baguio Market. These former headhunters can sometimes be seen heavily tattooed and wearing traditional handwoven clothing.

The city sprawls over thirty square miles, with winding roads that follow the contours of the land. The tall pine trees that cover the mountains sing in the night wind that rushes down the deep canyons beyond the city. In the morning, there is a light mist that carries the scent of fragrant vegetation. The world-famous, 2,000-year-old, stone-walled rice terraces at Banaue are just north of Baguio.

The city has five universities, a military academy, a country club, a large cathedral, a botanical and zoological garden, and a centrally-located park with a lake. Baguio is famous for strawberries and artisans who make silver filigree jewelry. The lush greenery and cool climate make it a major destination for foreigners and affluent Filipinos seeking a break from the heat of the lowlands. Baguio is often called the *Summer Capital* because so many people from Manila live there during the dry season. I am looking forward to a cool, quiet hotel room, where I can think clearly about the events of the past few weeks.

The bus stops at the terminal not far from the center of town. Descending the stairs with the other passengers, I feel a light breeze. As it brushes my check, I am amazed at how much I appreciate the sensation after being in an environment where the humidity is so stifling that nothing moves and the cost of running an electric fan is prohibitive—an environment where it is better to lie in bed most of the day and take small, measured breaths to avoid further exhaustion.

Shouldering my backpack, I walk along Session Road through a busy commercial district filled with throngs of students until I reach the Baguio Market, which takes up an entire city block. Two blind musicians are standing on the concrete steps with several small children playing at their feet. Obviously man and wife, they are singing what sounds like Pentecostal music—him on guitar; her with a broken tambourine; both off-key. The man's unseeing, white-filmed eyes roll from left to right, and then up towards the sky as he sways his head in time with the music.

Dropping a few coins into the tin cup attached to his instrument, I enter the market. Although the outside street stalls are vibrant and teeming with shoppers, and the first floor is filled with people eating at small restaurants serving cheap food, a blanket of dusty silence descends over me when I enter the upper levels of the building. Ancient wooden planks creak beneath my feet, as I wander through three floors of shops offering a wide selection of handicrafts: baskets, blankets, sweaters, household goods, wood carvings, antiques, and jewelry.

Leaving the market several hours later—my backpack now heavy with fifty-year-old, polished and worn coconut shell bowls, three hand-carved, wooden angels, each playing a tiny musical instrument, the tooth of a wild pig, and antlers from a mountain deer—I begin to make my way towards the *Swagman Attic Hotel*. I have chosen the Swagman based on advertising: 24-hour restaurant and bar, fans in every room, hot water in the showers, and working telephones.

After renting a room for the peso equivalent of $20 a night, I lie on the bed in a dimly-lit room under a whirling ceiling fan. The complexity of my relationships with Joseph, Mely, and the other people I have met in Vacante swirls in my head, keeping rhythm with the fan, until I fall into a deep sleep filled with darting shadows, conflicting desires, and threatening questions. Someone chases me in a dream, and although I am afraid, part of me wants to be caught.

It is late in the evening when I awake, perhaps 10:00 P.M., and I am hungry. After walking several blocks, I discover a restaurant called simply *The 50's Diner*. The outer façade and interior are painted hot pink with turquoise trim. Elvis is playing on the jukebox, and high on the far wall hangs the front third of a 1953 Chevy. The menu consists of mostly hamburgers, French fries, and milkshakes.

I slip into a booth with black vinyl seats, and the waitress arrives to take my order. She is wearing white lace-up roller skates and a miniskirt. When she rolls out through the swinging kitchen doors twenty minutes later and careens towards me on her skates while carrying a serving tray loaded with food, I am not sure whether I should laugh or dive under the table for safety.

Later, while walking down a narrow side street around midnight on my way back to the Swagman, I notice a stocky man with blond hair and blue eyes standing idly in the street. He looks to be about 25 years old, and he is the first person with white skin I have seen in several weeks.

"Hello. Do you speak English?" I say.

"Yes, good evening, miss," he responds with a thick German accent. Then, more hesitantly, "Would you like to share a beer?"

Intrigued by the thought of a conversation in English, I nod my head "Yes," and we enter the closest doorway, which turns out to be the entrance to the *Cuckoo's Nest Folkhouse*. Inside, students from the local college are having a boisterous party. The middle-aged proprietor welcomes us graciously and offers us beer. Settling into a quiet corner we exchange stories.

"My name is Ramon. I am from Munich, Germany."

"And I am Jessica from California."

His eyes dart around the room. He resembles a frightened bird. His face droops slightly at the edges, but he is smiling.

"I have come to the Philippines in search of a wife. Everyone back home in Germany told me I was crazy. They said I would be beaten and robbed by Filipino gangsters. Even the guidebooks say to be careful of strangers, but not you, because you are from the United States."

Thinking of my own experiences with the Naces family in Vacante, I ask, "Do you have any friends in the Philippines? A family who will sponsor you?"

"No. I have not met anyone, and I am here already one week. This is my first real conversation and you are not even Filipino. I'm thinking of hiring a personal bodyguard to escort me.

"Otherwise, how will I ever find a wife?"

Struck by the sadness of Ramon's situation, I spontaneously offer an invitation: "Please visit me and my friends next weekend. We will have a party. Also, there is a church where they have a faith healer," I say, thinking to myself, *He certainly needs healing, if only to help him relax.*

"Hello, Miss. Are you new to Baguio?" The proprietor has joined us, bringing more beer, this time at no charge.

"I am from California and my companion is from Germany. I am a folksinger."

"Well then, you must sing for us. Tonight we celebrate the seventh anniversary of Filipino Independence."

A young man is banging away on a worn guitar. He hands me the instrument, and soon I am deep into the energy of the party. "We Shall Overcome" and "Get Together" (the '60s anthem recorded by the Youngbloods) are the only songs I can think of that are even remotely related to independence and cultural unity. But the noisy audience—which has probably never heard these songs anyway—reacts with enthusiastic applause.

When I return to the table, Ramon seems more at ease. "Yes, I will visit Vacante. Please write for me the directions," he says.

The Miracle
and the Enigma

The First Psychic Surgeon: Eleuterio Terte

Psychic surgery in the Philippines developed within the Union. The first Espiritista medium to practice this dramatic form of healing was Eleuterio Terte, who was born in 1905 in San Fabian, Pangasinan, to parents who were deeply involved with the Union. Harvey Martin writes about Terte, saying:

"Despite his religious upbringing, Terte showed no interest in spiritual matters. In 1927, he nearly died from a terrible illness. He had a dream during the course of his illness. Close to death and suffering from a high fever, two angels appeared and offered to heal him on the condition that he would, in turn, heal others. He agreed to become a healer, and upon recovering from his illness, he was baptized and initiated into the community of Christian Spiritists. During his baptism service, the presiding medium revealed that Terte had been chosen by God to heal through magnetic healing and laying on of hands. Subsequently, Terte's reputation as a healer spread and soon his renowned healing ability brought hundreds of patients to his small village." (15)

Continued on page 118.

Mock Wedding

No awan ti tinapay, cancanen ket nasaysayaat pay.
If there is no bread, native cakes are even better.

Rosa has baked an enormous cake for Joseph's birthday using cassava fruit, molasses, milk from green coconuts, and sweet rice. The fragrance fills the small house. About twenty people, mostly women and children, are sitting in a large circle in the center of the living room. The young women fidget in their seats and giggle from behind raised palms because Ramon from Germany has joined us for the weekend. He is very large compared to everyone else and also very white. His blue eyes seem to light up the entire room.

The party begins tentatively, but soon everyone is joking and teasing Joseph about getting older. Someone announces that each person must sing. Many of them are so shy they either shake their heads, indicating they will not "perform," or their contribution is mumbled and indecipherable.

Eventually, Ramon's turn comes around. At first he is speechless. Finally, he says hesitantly, "In Germany I did not learn any love songs, only military songs."

I think he actually said "...there are no love songs in Germany," but this couldn't possibly be true, could it? It appears he has come to the correct conclusion that the Filipinos are a deeply romantic people, and since he doesn't know a love song, he will not have to sing one.

"Well, then. Sing us a military song," says Luna emphatically, not willing to let the opportunity for a joke to pass without comment.

Staring at his feet so he will not have to meet anyone's eyes, Ramon begins to sing awkwardly in German. His voice is coarse—as if this is the first time he has used it for singing in many years. The song is definitely militaristic, moving to the rhythm of aggressively marching feet.

The easily-imagined image of soldiers carrying rifles is so completely out of context here in Vacante that everyone begins to laugh. Soon Ramon, too, is laughing. The sound begins deep in his body and rumbles up higher and higher until he explodes in a near fit, which only makes everyone else roar even louder.

Someone turns on the tape player and pushes the chairs aside for dancing. Joseph takes my hand, and holding me tightly he whirls me out into the center of the room. Leaning closer for a brief moment, he whispers in my ear, "I want to kiss you."

He was wearing gold-colored corduroy pants and a pressed white shirt. His wife, Rosa, stood silently in the corner near the cake wringing her hands. But I didn't know what to do. I couldn't stop myself from wanting to be close to him.

◦◦◅▦▻◦◦

The circle gathers around us to watch, and someone puts a tattered handkerchief on top of my head. Not understanding this gesture, I continue dancing with Joseph. Soon everyone else is dancing, too.

When the music ends, we are once again left standing in the middle of the room. I still have the hanky on my head. One old lady takes an empty dinner plate and circles the room, holding it out to each person. One by one, they each pretend to put something on the plate. Considering this to be some strange Filipino ritual, I ignore them and begin cutting the cake, which is light and creamy, and filled with the flavors of Pangasinan.

Afterwards, when everyone begins to drift back to their own places, Joseph walks with me to the nipa hut.

"What were they doing with the handkerchief? Why did some-one pass around a plate?"

"They were pretending we got married. The hanky was your special veil, and the plate was passed around for money. This is what we do at wedding parties."

With my back against the nipa hut, where no one can see us, he presses his body against mine, and I feel the softness of his lips as Joseph gives me his wedding kiss. Then he quickly slips away, leaving me trembling in the shadows.

The next day, Sunday, we are all back in the church for services. Ramon sits in the front pew, his eyes glued to the speaker, even though he does not understand a word of the language. Everyone else is struggling to pay attention to the sermon, but they would much rather stare at Ramon. They are still captivated by his large body and blue eyes.

Mely rises from her chair: "Today, we have an honored guest from Germany. Ramon, please come to the front and address the congregation."

No one expected this, certainly not Ramon. He shuffles slowly up to the podium and after clearing his throat, he bursts into tears.

"Even though I am twenty-three years old, I never learned how to laugh. Thank you for teaching me how to laugh. I will never forget you," he says.

The Miracle
and the Enigma

John Huddleston, who has participated in guided tours to the Philippines for spiritual study and visits to various faith healers, also describes Terte's development:

"During World War II, Terte was captured by the Japanese. It was during this period that his gift of what would later be called *psychic surgery* began to manifest. He found he was able to cause the wounds inflicted by his captors to heal spontaneously. Terte was a trance medium who used his body as a vehicle through which he channeled the healing power of spirit. After the war, these healing guides began to change the nature of his healings. Terte found he could raise the vibration of his body through prayer, and when the vibration was high enough his guide would enter his body and raise the energy of his hands even higher. At this point, his hands were actually able to penetrate a patient's body to perform healing." (17)

Continued on page 129.

The Saltmakers of Bolinao

⊶⋖⊛⋗⊷

Ang masama ay tumatakas nang walang taong humahabol.
The evil one flees even if not pursued.

After the visit with Ramon, Mely announces we are going on another mission, this time to consecrate a new church built by Trinidad's brother-in-law, Marcos Sisteron. The next morning, Mely, Trinidad, Luna, Joseph and I, and several others drive to Bolinao in the jeepney.

The town of Bolinao, in the Hundred Islands region of Pangasinan, is on a peninsula that juts out into the South China Sea and the Gulf of Lingayen. The local people support themselves by fishing, extracting salt from sea water, and collecting shells on the beach to make household items and souvenirs for tourists. Chinese junks and Mexican galleons laden with treasure are said to be sunken offshore. Important archaeological discoveries have been made here, and the area is also associated with unexpected paranormal phenomena, including strange lights in the night sky.

The Church of St. James in Bolinao is one of the oldest Catholic churches in the Philippines, built in 1609. Constructed from stone blocks and surrounded by tall palm trees, there are plants growing out of the roof and moss in the cracks between the stones. The thick wooden planks of the floors are worn smooth from centuries of use. The building appears to be a living, breathing entity. Priests still hold services here, but the church has also sheltered the townspeople from pirate attacks and during war. The wooden statutes of saints and an altar flanked by two grinning Aztec-like faces with protruding tongues reflect the former ties of the Philippines with Mexico.

The Sisteron family lives on an island that lies a short distance off Cape Bolinao, but before departing by boat we visit Trinidad's mother, who lives in a two-room, wooden hut in the center of the village. A soft rustling sound comes from inside when we knock on the door. After a few minutes, the door opens and a young woman peeks out. "Please, to wait," she says. "Mother will be with you in a moment, but first she must put on her Sunday dress."

When the door opens again, the tiniest old woman I have ever seen appears. She is wearing a slightly rumpled, bright blue dress with yellow flowers, and she seems lost inside of it.

"Mabuhay, Mabuhay," she says, offering us a whispered welcome as we enter her modest home.

Trinidad begins to flit nervously around the room, talking loudly. She has not seen her mother in a long time and hopes we will make a good impression. Trinidad offers us seats in tall-backed, bamboo chairs, and the young girl serves cookies and glasses of lukewarm tea.

The old woman sits silently amidst the flurry. Smelling vaguely of mothballs, she seems shocked by my presence. Even though I am only five feet, two inches tall, I am a foot taller than she is. I must seem like a giant, and she stares at me speechless. But this awkward beginning is broken when I take out my guitar and start singing a lively song. Much to my surprise, the old woman rises from her chair and begins to dance in the center of the room, taking cautious steps and twirling around in a slow circle. Once again, music has transcended our lack of common language.

She dances for only a few moments and then sits back down. As if to return my gift of music, she begins to sing a Filipino love song—and her voice is like the wind rustling in pampas grass, so soft it can hardly be heard. She sings just one stanza, smiles at me, and announces she is going to the kitchen to prepare our food. Trinidad says her mother also does her own washing and is quite proud of it. When I pick up my camera to take a photo of her ancient face, she reaches out to hug me and then buries her face in my neck for a moment before leaving the room.

Trinidad's mother was 113 years old at the time of our meeting. Sometime after I returned to Berkeley, I received a letter saying she had died peacefully in her sleep at the age of 118.

Next, we make our way down to a small bay, where Marcos Sisteron is waiting for us. After eating lunch at the dock, we get into his long, narrow, *banca* boat. He asks me to sit in the middle because I am the heaviest passenger. The boat is shaped like a canoe, with an arrangement of bamboo poles that stick out sideways. These poles, together with two center vertical poles, hold the sails. But today they are rolled up because the wind is weak and the boat must be powered by a small motor. The smell of the sea and the coolness of a slight breeze wash over us as we glide easily through the water.

When we arrive at the island, Marcos skillfully steers the boat between large, open places at the edge of the shore. About fifteen feet square, they are bounded by foot-high mounds of mud. These are the saltwater evaporation ponds of the Sisteron family. Water is retained in the ponds when the tide goes out, and after the water has evaporated in the sun, the remaining salt is collected and cleaned by hand.

There are about eight ponds, and as the boat pulls up to the edge of the outermost one, a cloud of flies lazy from the hot sun rises and circles in response to our arrival. Balancing our bags carefully, we walk on the top of one of the dried mud ridges until we are on solid ground, the rich, pungent odor of rotting plant and sea life all around us.

The family lives in a circle of six nipa huts in the middle of a thick jungle. It is still the dry season and everything is covered with a thin layer of brown dust. There is an outdoor kitchen with a table and chairs, and a roof-less "comfort room" hidden behind thin walls of nipa grass. At one edge of the circle is a monolithic stone structure that seems to grow out of the volcanic rock of the island. This is Mr. Sisteron's new church. The sandy-white color of the rough-textured stone is contrasted against the green of the surrounding trees and the blue sky. The building seems rather grandiose and awkward compared to the family's humble nipa huts, and it reminds me of a scene from a movie, perhaps *Raiders of the Lost Ark*.

While Joseph carries our bags to the guest quarters, Luna and I climb the steep, stone stairs until we are standing inside the sanctuary. The room is simple and airy, and the sun shines down through openings in the roof—perhaps the building is not finished or the roof is made of loosely woven grass that allows light to enter.

The largest object in the sanctuary is a twelve-foot long, wooden altar covered with candles, religious pictures, and statutes. A painting of an eye within a triangle hangs above it. This is the largest painting of this type I have ever seen, about five feet square. It seems somehow ominous—as if the eye is looking directly at me, piercing me. My breath quickens and my palms begin to sweat.

Turning away, I notice a room attached to the stone building at the same level; this is the guest quarters. The structure is made of wood, and is reached by climbing a ladder or entering through the door connecting it to the church. Luna and I enter and decide to take a nap. A cool breeze flows gently up through the floor of slatted bamboo, and soon the others have joined us for an afternoon siesta.

I am awakened by Luna, who is shaking my shoulder because it is time for dinner. Descending the rickety ladder, I see a fire has been made in the center of the clearing. A bamboo tube about three feet long and four inches thick sits suspended on two forked sticks above the coals. Inside this tube is a mixture of coconut milk, molasses, and sweet rice—the same kind of dessert that was served at Joseph's birthday party.

The thick, taffy-like cake is spooned onto my plate, to be eaten without utensils, its delicate fragrance mixing with the smoke of the fire. I am also offered fried chicken, but the poor bird must have starved to death because there is almost no meat on its bones. Everyone watches to see whether I approve of the food, and they smile when I compliment the cook. Joseph hovers nearby watching me, but never touching and seldom speaking.

The conversation is animated as old friends and families are reunited. As usual, they speak in the local dialect, but from the sound of their voices I can tell they are worried. Mr. and Mrs. Sisteron are frowning and Mely is nodding her head sympathetically. When I pull her aside and ask what they are talking about, she answers vaguely that there is a problem with someone from outside the family.

Soon darkness falls and there is no moon. Taking a small flashlight from my pocket, I make my way towards the toilet at the far end of the communal area. Stumbling, I am surprised when Joseph appears from out of the darkness and grabs my arm to keep me from falling.

"Come with me," he whispers, leading me towards a narrow path.

After walking for about ten minutes, we arrive at a fishing pier. We sit dangling our feet in the water and talking about wanting to have a life together, and his dreams of working on a farm in California for decent wages.

I knew he wanted to be with me, but I also knew he wanted a life free of economic struggle. Like many people living in Third World countries, he would do almost anything to break free of his limited circumstances.

❖

On the way back, Joseph suddenly pulls me off the path and into the jungle.

"Lie down," he says.

This from a man who just yesterday put three fingers into the vagina of his pig and said: "She's ready," before loading the squealing, resistant pig onto a cart to be taken somewhere and impregnated by one of three potential "boyfriends."

"Lie down," he says again.

The earth beneath me seems to rise up, encouraging me to surrender to his command, and our bodies are drawn together in a natural embrace. He is sweet and musky, and soft with an inner power.

An invisible barrier has been broken, a chasm crossed. I have become large, expanded, stretched far beyond the fertile valleys of Pangasinan. There is a sense of belonging to him and the land beneath us. The demarcation line between love and the need to hide it has become blurred. But, still, there is confusion. Am I in danger? Will there be repercussions? Although I am afraid, it is also terribly exciting. Somehow, I need to create space for him in my real life, not just in this lucid dream world on an island in the South Pacific.

Rising, he takes my hand, and we follow the jungle path back towards the others, stopping only to kiss briefly before entering separately into the light of the fire. A blanket of silence falls around us as we leave the reality of our brief joining and are reabsorbed back into the place where we are almost strangers. I become a shadow, an illusion, a delusion. I am no longer my authentic self.

I mumble something to Luna about getting lost while trying to find the toilet, but she gives no indication she suspects anything.

Watching Joseph across the fire, the impossibility of our relationship falls heavily upon me. Almost immediately, I begin to regret the episode in the jungle and the conflict it creates. If I try hard enough, perhaps I can forget it.

Satiated with dinner and tired from the activities of the day, one by one, each person departs for their sleeping place. Climbing the ladder, I find my bedroll and lie there thinking of Joseph at the other end of the room. I imagine he is wishing we could be together. Soon, heavy with heat and rice cake, and my indigestible thoughts, I sleep fitfully.

Sometime around midnight, a bell begins to ring inside the church. Accompanied by soft whispering and perhaps chanting, it lasts about ten minutes. As far as I can tell, no one but me wakes up, and I fall asleep again when the noise stops.

Again at two o'clock, the annoying bell.

And again at four.

And yet again at six, when I rise from the floor totally pissed off at the idiot who has kept me awake most of the night. In a daze, I make my way down the ladder and find Mely alone, drinking coffee.

"What was that horrible ringing?" I say, thinking it must be some unusual Filipino religious custom.

"A stranger from Manila has been here for many weeks making trouble," Mely explains. "He will not let the family rest. He insists they must pray in the church when he rings the bell, but only one girl obeys."

"Why doesn't someone tell him to leave?"

"Oh no, they cannot speak to him. He has cast a strong spell, and they are afraid." Mely nods in the direction of the man. He is standing at the top of the church steps and glaring down at us in a probable attempt to look like a person of some authority.

He seems rather ordinary to me, not supernatural at all, and certainly not capable of casting a "spell." But even Marcos Sisteron, who was able to build a stone church, appears to be impotent in dealing with this troublemaker.

Perhaps he is a psychic vampire, who needs them to pray at night when they are the most vulnerable so he can drain them of their life force. Maybe he needs their energy to survive. He could be "mangkukulam," intent on doing evil. According to Filipino superstition, mangkukulam are aligned with the devil and are quite powerful, although they are scared of healers like Mely. Some of them do weird things to hurt others, such as putting pieces of plastic or insects inside the bodies of their victims. They also stick pins in dolls, similar to voodoo practitioners.

◦○◄✦►○◦

"Do you want me to say something to him? I'm not afraid," I tell Mely.

"Oh no. It would be impolite to interfere."

Evidently, she is planning to deal with the situation diplomatically, as is the Filipino custom. But at that moment, a more concrete plan begins to form in my mind.

After breakfast—rice again with a small mouthful of fish—a discussion begins about how to entertain the "tourist from America." Finally, the Sisterons decide they will take me to another island to pick fresh coconuts.

While everyone prepares to leave, I climb the ladder to our sleeping room and enter the church from the side door. The bell is sitting prominently in the center of the altar. After making sure no one can see me, I put it under my shirt and take it back to my bedroll, where I hide it under my pillow. *There! Now we will be able to sleep undisturbed. And I won't tell anyone, not even Joseph. What a great joke to play on the "warlock" from Manila.*

◦○◄✦►○◦

"You will like very much the young coconuts," says Mrs. Sisteron, as we get into the boat carrying baskets of food for a picnic. When we arrive at a neighboring island, the anchor is laid about fifty yards from the shore because the water is so shallow.

"Let's go," says Luna. She and Joseph leap out of the boat shoe-less, but I hesitate because I am worried about what might lie beneath the cloudy water. As I am putting on my sandals, I hear Luna cry out. She is holding up her bleeding foot, which has been cut by coral.

After wrapping her foot in leaves, we walk up a short incline through thick jungle until we arrive in the middle of a grove of coconut trees, their graceful, green branches bending in the breeze far above us. While the adults recline on a raised bamboo platform and eat lunch, two young boys quickly climb far up into the trees. Like all of the males in this "tribe," they have strangely-shaped feet, with toes that are widely spread and a big toe that works like an opposable thumb. This most likely evolved over generations to facilitate the easy climbing of coconut trees.

Shinnying down feet first, one of the boys approaches me and after carefully cutting a hole in a large brown coconut, he silently hands it to me so I can suck out the delicious milk.

Joseph watches from a short distance away. My pulse quickens when he looks in the direction of a small stand of trees about fifty yards up the beach. His eyes dart several times from my face to the edge of the water and back. *He wants me to follow him.* No one else seems to observe this silent interaction, and we begin to drift casually along the shore, separately, at first. Walking behind him, I pause now and then to pick up a piece of coral or a shell and put it in my pocket.

After a few minutes, the beach curves sharply to the right, and we reach a place where no one can see us. Stopping abruptly, he moves towards me. Our embrace is immediate and intense. We lay together on the sand, hidden by tall sea grass with a cloudless sky above, the warmth of the sun on our skin, and the sound of the ocean just a few feet away. He begins to kiss me, and for a few moments I am water flowing without boundaries. I am caressed by the sweetness of molasses.

But there is not enough time because we are afraid of raising suspicion. All too soon, we are walking slowly back along the edge of the water again, separate, not touching. Inside I am delirious with desire, even though outwardly I must pretend I feel nothing out of the ordinary. The others are still eating lunch when we arrive back at the grove of coconut trees. If they questioned our absence, no one says anything or even looks at us. *I wonder if I will I ever get used to hiding my feelings for him in front of the others?*

One of the teenage boys has been carving a bowl from half of a coconut shell all morning, carefully removing the hairy outer skin and inner pulp. "Here, miss, I made this for you," he says, handing it to me to take home as a souvenir.

There is no fresh water on the island, and I have only one gallon of bottled water with me because I did not know we would be staying for three days. It will have to be carefully rationed, which is not easy in 90-degree weather. This also means there is no fresh water for bathing. As if reading my mind, Mely announces we are going to a third island to take a bath. The picnic things are gathered up, and soon we are back in the boat.

When we arrive at the next island, I discover the "bath" is a rock-lined pool fed by a natural spring. Taking off my dress to the sound of muffled snickering, I enter the pool and sit cross-legged in the slightly warm water wearing only my undershirt and panties. The floor of the pool is made of soft, welcoming sand. A grinning, middle-aged woman also gets in and sits across from me, just a few feet away. She has one tooth in her mouth—on the top, just under her nose. A large group of people gathers around us, pretending not to stare.

The woman smiles and hands me a small piece of soap. As we begin to wash our upper bodies, an unspoken communication flies between us—we are both thinking the same thing. The surrounding crowd leans forward, their breathing suspended, because somehow they, too, know I want to wash my crotch.

My bathing partner winks at me and quickly thrusts her hand into the water and into her underpants. *At least I think she was wearing underpants. I hope so—although her bulbous, brown breasts were naked and floating on the water between us.* Without hesitation, my own hand dives into the water, and we begin washing between our legs. The spell broken, the expectant crowd roars with laughter.

Later that night, lying on the hard bamboo floor back at the Sister-on's, the only sounds to be heard are the singing of the night birds, the buzz of the cicadas as they rub their legs together in unison, the distant barking of a dog, and the gentle breathing of the other sleepers. These are sounds that soothe and caress as I drift into sleep, savoring the remembered taste of Joseph's mouth on mine as we lay together on the heated sand under bright sun. Nothing can be seen in the darkness except a sliver of moon shining in through the glass-less windows.

◦─◁▣✳▣▷─◦

At breakfast the next morning, Mely is unusually talkative: "The man from Manila is gone. He left early this morning because his bell disappeared. He said it was a sign from God that he should go." She imparts this information with great seriousness, but I can also see amusement in her eyes. "Everyone is very happy, except for one girl. She is crying in her room," Mely adds.

Feeling guilty, I confess: "It was me. I hid the bell so we could sleep."

Hearing this, Mely turns away, her face expressionless, which makes it difficult to tell how she feels about what I have done. Perhaps I have broken some protocol related to politeness. After breakfast, however, she says it is time for me to receive healing in the church, so she must not be too upset. Trinidad comes with us to assist.

Lying half-naked on a narrow table, I gaze at the dust motes floating dreamily in the morning sun high in the center of the sanctuary. The Eye of the Holy Spirit seems to stare down at us. When Mely thrusts her hand deep into my lower abdomen, there is some pain from the pressure of her searching fingers. Finally, she pulls out a small, bloody mass about the size of a large walnut.

"Here," she says. "This is the root of your sorrow."

It makes a resounding ring when she drops it into a metal basin.

"Jessica. It's hard like a stone," exclaims Trinidad.

The Miracle
and the Enigma

In addition to being the first Espiritista medium to perform a psychic operation, Terte used a circular disc to locate fresh water on Tambac Island off the coast at Bolinao, where there was insufficient water for the salt harvesters. He pointed to a particular spot and said, "Over there you'll find water. You will dig hard, you'll find rock, but keep on digging. After you've found that rock, you'll find fresh water. And if you have the well blessed, that's going to be medicinal water." Water was, indeed, found at that spot.

Terte always carried the Bible with him. He began performing spirit-directed psychic surgery in the late 1940s. Apparently accepting his role completely, Terte said, "A healer can't stop healing the sick because that is his mission." (18)

Within a few years, many others were healing in the same way. Each of them told of a similar experience. They began as ministers of the Union, and then the Holy Spirit would appear in a vision and "give them the gift of healing." Many healers have since left the Union and formed their own churches.

Continued on page 132.

Dual Realities

◦◦━━━✳━━━◦◦

Kon owa it paghili-uyon, owa man it kalinong.
When there is no understanding, there is no peace.

"Kiss me the way you kiss Joseph," says Luna.

She is lying on the bed, and I am sitting next to her. A smile plays at the corner of her mouth; her black hair flows over the white of the pillowcase. She twists her body slightly, thrusting up her right hip. We are in her room discussing the concept of "dual realities," except we do not call it by that name, only "what happens during psychic surgery."

I am momentarily stunned. In a way it seems perfectly natural to lean over and try it as an experiment. But I have never kissed a girl in *that* way; nor has the opportunity ever arisen before.

Luna continues to lie there gazing up at me with her large brown eyes, her skin smooth and soft, her teeth white, her eyelashes long and delicate. She reminds me of a small kitten that rolls over and throws up its legs, begging to have its belly tickled.

"Kiss me the way you kiss Joseph."

Her words ring in my ears. Perhaps she is testing me, trying to find out if I have, indeed, kissed her brother and broken a family taboo. The attraction between Joseph and me seems almost palpable, and sometimes I feel as if Luna and the others are riveted to our every move and nuance of emotion. Then, again, perhaps she has never kissed anyone and is merely curious to see what it feels like.

The awkward moment passes, and we begin talking again about psychic surgery and the idea of dual realities. The requested kiss forgotten, she does not appear to be concerned. We are trying to answer a metaphysical question: "How can two seemingly opposite things be true at the same time?" For example: One person kisses another. The same person does not kiss another. So, was there a kiss?

Another example: In the world of energy and spirit, a tumor has been removed—the "root of my sorrow," as Mely described it—meaning the energy that creates and sustains the tumor is gone. But in the dimension of physical reality and common experience the tumor has *not* been removed, nor has it dissolved. The question is an endless Gordian knot inside my head. It goes around and around until I am dizzy.

I have just returned from Bolinao and my healing with Mely. The pain and pressure in my lower belly is completely gone. I feel empty and light. But, during an examination in Binalonan this morning the doctor said, "Sorry, miss, but you have a small fibroid tumor."

So what was removed? What made the sound in the bowl when Mely dropped it there? How can I both have a tumor, yet not have a tumor? I have read that the physical body needs time to catch up to the healing of the etheric body, but how long will it take? And will I have the necessary patience?

Luna's soft voice rises and falls like notes on a musical scale. In the sing-song lilt of English spoken by a Filipino, she sums up the situation: "Have Faith in GOD. He will give you un-der-*stand*-ing. Only He has the power to remove sickness."

The Miracle
and the Enigma

The Most Famous Psychic Surgeon: Tony Agpaoa

Born in 1939, Tony Agpaoa exhibited mystical powers even as a child when, at the age of ten, he began to heal his playmates of bleeding wounds. He was also said to be able to vanish from one place and reappear in another without warning. Born into a poor family in Rosales, Pangasinan, and having no formal education, he eventually became a healer who was sought after by thousands of ordinary people as well as princes and kings.

Agpaoa's unusual abilities were publicized in Harold Sherman's book *The Wonder Healers of the Philippines.* (19) As a result, he was interviewed, tested, analyzed, and experimented on by scientists from around the world. No one was ever able to prove him guilty of trickery, and some experts even declared him to be capable of genuine miracles. Tony Agpaoa was a colorful and effective healer, and when he died in 1982, many said it was the death of a legend.

Jaime T. Licauco discusses Agpaoa in *The Magicians of God*: "Tony said that the philosophy of healing is the most important thing to realize in the healing process. The healer must be concerned with the three bodies of man, not just the physical. By the three bodies, he meant the physical, the astral (or energy body), and the spiritual. He believed that unless a healer is able to heal the three bodies, he will be ineffective. That's why he considered the mental and spiritual preparation, or attunement, of the patients prior to treatment vital to a successful healing." (5)

Continued on page 140.

Leaving

Bisan ngain an tadong, mauli ha kalugaringon.
Wherever a man goes, in the end he comes home.

During the days leading up to my departure, I felt suffocated within the confines of Vacante. Joseph and I spent hours sitting on the porch of the nipa hut, singing sad songs and trying to frame our possible future. It was difficult to admit my feelings, even to myself, but I knew I was not the first woman to fall in love with a married man.

Tina issued a warning: "Jessica, your skin is so white we can see you in the dark. You glow like the flame of an oil lamp."

So I lay in bed behind the unlocked door of the nipa hut, waiting for Joseph's soft foot on the darkened stairs and the hurried tenderness of his touch. But he came only twice, entering silently like a thief.

He continued to insist he was not *really* married to Rosa, because his uncle never filed the marriage certificate. We even drove to City Hall in Binalonan, only to find out that Joseph was, in fact, officially married. Divorce is not allowed in the Philippines, so we devised a plan to obtain a tourist visa. When he arrived in California, he would divorce Rosa and marry me.

Was I crazy? Delusional? Had the oppressive heat of the lowlands addled my brain? What did I think I was going to do with a rice farmer in Berkeley?

The night before I was scheduled to leave, Mely and I talked about the economics of my staying in the Philippines. One idea was to open a restaurant in Binalonon. I would be the manager, she would do the cooking, and Trinidad would wash the dishes. Alternatively, I could buy a motorcycle, have it converted to public transport as a tricycle, and hire someone to drive it. In the end, we decided I could not stay, mostly because of my inability to tolerate hot weather, but Mely made me promise I would not forget her and her family. She asked me to visit as often as possible.

I packed my suitcase, taking with me a bag of coarse, slightly sweet salt (a gift from Marcos Sisteron), coral from the beach at Bolinao, several coconut shell bowls, three hand-carved wooden angels, a pig's tooth, deer antlers, and a jar filled with fresh molasses, a gift from Joseph.

Sleepy and with heavy hearts, Joseph and I drove to the main highway at 4:00 A.M. Rosa's brother, Andy, went with us as a chaperone. While we waited on the empty road for the bus that would take me to the airport in Manila, Andy discretely turned his head away and pretended to be asleep. Joseph's hands were clammy and his eyes wet when we kissed goodbye. We did not know when we would see each other again.

Tears rolled down my cheeks, as I took a seat at the rear of the bus. The old man in the seat next to me was gently snoring, and across the aisle someone was eating breakfast from a plastic bag, filling the air with the smell of dried fish. Lost in the limbo of the bus, I detached from everything around me. I became two different versions of myself, the past and the future, yet I was really nowhere at all. Everything, including my own identity, began to slowly dissolve as I moved out of the vibrational energy vortex of Pangasinan. It was as if the place itself existed in a paranormal reality or different dimension.

When I reached the airport, the cloudiness in my head began to dissipate, perhaps because of the air-conditioning, and I was able to think clearly for the first time in weeks. Unexpectedly, the intensity of my experience in the lowlands with Joseph and the others began to fade, losing color and passion.

Finally, after boarding the plane, I was back in the immediacy of the present moment, which no longer included Vacante. I tried to think about my life back in the States, but I could hardly remember it, focusing instead on the smiling stewardesses and the rolling cart that moved up and down the aisle bringing drinks and food.

Return to Pangasinan

Balikbayan Boxes

Kinsa kadtong maka hulat, maka kuha sa iyang guipangandoy.
He who knows how to wait can get what he desires.

I returned to the Philippines nine months later, after receiving a troubling letter from Belen saying Mely was bedridden with ovarian cancer. *She must have been sick when I saw her in March. Why didn't she tell me? How could I not have noticed?*

I booked a flight for just before my birthday in mid-December, and even though I arrived early at the international terminal of the San Francisco airport, there were already hundreds of people waiting in long lines at the check-in counters. There were piles of suitcases as far as I could see in any direction—and large cardboard boxes imprinted with the words *"BALIKBAYAN BOX."*

These boxes are usually about three feet square and filled with merchandise. Transporting them is a major industry worldwide because so many Filipinos live overseas. *Balikbayan* means "to return home," and the boxes are used to ship such things as toys, clothing, electronics, small appliances, chocolate, Spam, toothpaste, shampoo, door knobs, and car parts to friends and family in the Philippines. The charges are often by size rather than weight. Even a refrigerator can be shipped, although it will likely be priced as the equivalent of three boxes. Building supplies as heavy as marble floor tiles are sometimes sent because the items are not available locally, or because foreign-made goods are considered to be of higher quality.

The large number of boxes at the airport was likely related to the fact that it was almost Christmas and my fellow passengers were bringing home gifts. I was also bringing gifts: fifteen pairs of fake diamond earrings for the women and teenage girls, stationary for Luna (to encourage her to write more often), a gold lamé dress for

Minchu, kazoos, crayons, and jumping rubber frogs for the children, and matching tie-dyed, hippie teeshirts for Joseph and his son.

⁍⁍⁍✳⁍⁍⁍

The plane lifted off around midnight. Eighteen hours later, I staggered from the relatively tranquil atmosphere of the plane and into the chaos of the Manila airport, only to be told that the luggage had been left behind in Honolulu when we stopped for fuel. The headwinds had been strong, and the extra weight prevented the plane from getting off the ground and flying safely.

As I made my way to the customer service desk for Philippines Airlines, all I could think about was Mely. Perhaps she was already dead, and I would never see her again. Worse yet, I might get to Vacante just as they were having her funeral.

When I got to the counter, I began pounding it with my fist and yelling at the clerk, but she only stared at me, frightened and unsure of what to say. The supervisor took over and said I would have to wait like everyone else for my bag to arrive on another plane. Forcing a smile, he gave me a payment voucher for Pension Natividad.

After a restless night spent lying in bed and staring at a whirling ceiling fan, I returned to the airport to pick-up my suitcase, still wearing the same, now dirty, clothing I had left home in thirty-two hours earlier.

It was about 90 degrees with 99.9 percent humidity in the airplane hanger where I waited with the other passengers. There were no food booths in that part of the airport, and the smell of the chemical toilet was intolerable. I took refuge in watching the birds circling high in the rafters. They seemed undisturbed by the human chaos below. Sweat ran in rivulets down the middle of my back as I observed the scene.

My bag was located somewhere inside one of twelve cargo containers. There were about a dozen workers to unload and stack the luggage and balikbayan boxes in the crowded hanger. The man in charge frowned as he scribbled hurriedly on a clipboard, periodically chewing on his lower lip while talking on a walkie-talkie.

As each item was taken off the trolley bringing it from the plane, the number identifying it was recorded on clipboards carried by clerks wearing identical blue polyester jumpsuits. From there, the number was transferred to a computer and then announced over a loudspeaker. Most of the passengers were Filipino, and they waited patiently, listening and checking their baggage claim tickets as each number was called.

Only two of the workmen were actually doing anything, and it took almost three hours to unload the first cargo container. The pile of suitcases and balikbayan boxes began to rise higher and higher around me. Finally, after about five hours, my green plastic suitcase surfaced at the top of the pile—flotsam floating on a sea of cardboard boxes—and I was released from the torment of the airport.

I hailed a taxi to take me directly to the bus station. From there, I caught an air-conditioned bus to Binalonan and then a tricycle to Vacante. I felt apprehensive of what lay ahead.

The Miracle
and the Enigma

Alex L. Orbito, Psychic Surgeon

Alex Orbito was born in 1940 in Cuyapo, near Manila, the fourteenth child in a family of poor tenant farmers. His parents, particularly his mother, were involved in the founding of the Spiritist movement in the Philippines. Thus, he was literally "born into Spiritism."

Alex had a normal childhood until the age of 14, when he became aware of the spirit world through his dreams. One night he dreamed that he had healed a neighbor woman of paralysis. Unknown to Alex, she experienced a similar dream that same night. She sent for him, and after he had prayed over her and massaged her limbs with oil, she stood up and walked. The news of this miracle spread quickly, and Alex soon became a sought-after healer. However, he became discouraged because he was unable to earn a living as a healer, and for a time he avoided it altogether, traveling and taking other jobs.

But then fate intervened: he was framed for a crime he did not commit and thrown in jail. The Lord came to Alex as a voice entreating him to heal. He agreed, and the next day he was freed from jail. However, he continued to ignore the calling to serve humanity, and eventually he became extremely sick. Again, he heard the Divine Voice. At that point, he accepted his mission without question.

Alex Orbito has performed thousands of successful healings, and he conducts seminars twice a year in the Philippines.

Continued on page 146.

A Friend Lies Dying

Ang dalita'y kung dumalaw, karaniwa'y sabay-sabay.
When sorrows come, they usually come all together.

When I enter the house, Luna is reading a letter to Mely and several visitors. The letter is from Spain. The writer first complains of pain in his leg, and then says there are three hundred people waiting for Mely to come to Spain and do healing. Three hundred. The number seems incomprehensible.

What is Mely thinking as she lies in bed, silently staring out the window in the direction of the front garden, her slender, delicate fingers resting lightly on the edge of the bed? The number must loom large in her mind—so many to be healed, but she has no strength.

Mely had an active life just a few months ago, but now she cannot even turn over unassisted because her stomach is so swollen with cancer. She has not eaten solid food in weeks, and her thighs are as thin as my wrists. Her bed sits in the middle of the living room and someone is always nearby.

In America, the end of life often comes in a hospital, nursing home, or hospice. But things are different here in Vacante, where everyone is a caregiver and illness is a family affair. Mely's relatives take turns sleeping on the living room floor and getting up when she needs help. Luna is with her almost every night for months, and there are dark circles under her eyes.

"How are you?" Mely whispers, her face barely recognizable

Turning to Luna, she adds, "Take good care of our guest."

Unable to think of anything appropriate to say, I summon the courage to take out my guitar and sing one of her favorite songs. She turns her head slowly toward the sound and manages a faint smile.

Everything feels closed in and oppressive. A new house has been built near the water pump, obscuring the view of the sugarcane fields, and the front garden is overgrown with weeds because no one is tending it. There is a high fence around Minchu's nipa hut, as though the family is hiding. I lock the door at night when I go to bed. It is a time of darkness, melancholy, and gloomy dampness.

During the day, Belen soaks medicinal leaves in warm water and lovingly places them on Mely's bare stomach. After dinner, we gather to pray and perform magnetic healing while someone holds an open Bible over Mely's head. We circle the bed, somber and determined, as we attempt to will renewed life into her failing body.

Ironically, a woman arrives from Germany, Elsa. She also has ovarian cancer, and has come to Mely for healing. *Communication between the rural Filipino provinces and foreign countries was difficult in the early 1990s, when these events took place, and there was no way Elsa could have known about Mely's illness.*

Trinidad says Elsa was in Baguio the previous year and was cheated out of her money by a phony healer. She is so weak she can hardly walk from her room at Belen's to Mely's house, which is only fifty feet away.

"People like Elsa make it very difficult for us. What if she dies at our place? The authorities will blame us," says Trinidad. She tells me to follow Elsa wherever she goes and hold her hand so she will not fall.

Elsa and Mely spend every afternoon together for ten days behind closed doors. No one is allowed to listen to their conversation, but I imagine Mely is preparing Elsa for her inevitable transition. Elsa leaves in a tricycle headed for the highway, alone and unaided.

∞⊷✳⊶∞

Joseph is still here. His visa for the States was denied by U.S. Immigration, even though I obtained a letter of recommendation from my Congressman. I made the mistake of sending the letter directly to Joseph instead of the U.S. Embassy in Manila. When he presented the letter with his visa application, they tore it up, declaring it was forged. This is our deep failure: prevented by circumstance and governmental bureaucracy from being together.

When he is not caring for Mely, Joseph works in his rice paddy or the fish pond left behind after the rainy season. We ignore each other as much as possible. There are no more midnight rendevous in the jungle or my room. We avoid speaking of our mutual disappointment, but his eyes reflect the sadness in my own.

The nipa hut has fallen into disrepair, and my room is now on the second floor of Belen's more substantial house. Bats fly in and out of the windows when I turn off the lights, and the soft rush of their wings is somehow comforting.

We gather in the church at midnight on Christmas Eve to eat spaghetti. The noodles are soggy and the cheese bland, but the attempt at gaiety and hospitality is genuine. Afterwards, presents are opened in the living room, with Mely watching. I pass out Fourth of July sparklers, and we dance around the room waving them. The children soon become sleepy and are carried home to bed. The next day there is a parade, and brightly decorated wagons drawn by carabao and filled with joyful children pass in front of the house.

<hr/>

Everyone respects the fact that Mely is *actively* dying. We speak in soft tones and try not to laugh too loudly in her presence. She seems peaceful and centered in her process. For Mely, the thin veil between the physical world and the dimension of spirit has grown even more transparent. Like the other psychic surgeons I have met, she moves fluidly between the different dimensions of reality. She does not fear death, because she is already partly there. She accepts her situation with equanimity. Mely's spiritual work is the same no matter where she is, whether in the physical body or in spirit.

But although Mely is at peace, everyone else is upset. We miss her active participation in daily life. Mely is our leader, and without her we wander aimlessly, trying to understand *why* she is dying. We want to *do something* to keep her with us.

"Why hasn't Mely gone to another healer?" I ask Trinidad, who is in the kitchen preparing lunch.

"She trusts only Marcos Orbito, and he is far away. The other healers charge too much money. They cheat the people and do not preach the gospel before healing. Mely does not agree with their ways."

Determined to help, I ask her where to find Marcos.

At six in the morning the next day, I am up to prepare for my trip on the bus with Estifanio Banao, one of the church elders. We are planning to visit the highly-respected minister and healer Monsignor Marcos Orbito at his church in Tarlac, about fifty miles south on the MacArthur Highway. I plan to tell him about Mely's illness and ask him to come to Vacante to see her, but I am also curious for myself because he is the psychic surgeon who initiated both Connie Arismende and Mely as healers.

Estifanio arrives at 8:00 A.M. wearing a white starched shirt and his Sunday trousers. His hair is neatly slicked back with pomade. He is about seventy years old and speaks formal, textbook English. Each word is enunciated precisely, and his speech is free of colloquialisms, idioms, and slang. Most Filipinos learn English in school, but in the provinces there is little opportunity to meet Americans or other English-speaking foreigners. Estifanio lives in a one-room hut with his wife of fifty years. They do not have a television, a radio, or even a telephone. Without exposure to spoken English, everything he says sounds like he is reading out of an old-fashioned book:

"Thrice previous have I had the esteemed honor to meet with Monsr. Marcos Orbito. Come, Sister Jessica, henceforth let us set about attending to his presence and flock together to strengthen our faith and unity in multiplicity."

After about an hour on the bus, we arrive at Tarlac. Alerting the bus driver to our stop, we descend to the road and are immediately overwhelmed by dust and heat. The eldest daughter of Marco Orbito meets us at the door to the family compound.

"I'm sorry you have come so far," she says. "But my father is in California on a mission and will not return for six months."

Hearing this, the ever-present smile on Estifanio's face quickly fades. He looks like he is about to burst into tears. Several people gather to have coffee with us, and they are sympathetic after learning the reason for our visit. Marcos Orbito's wife promises that when her husband calls from the U.S. she will tell him about Mely's illness. Thirty minutes later, we are back on the road waiting for the return bus.

The Miracle
and the Enigma

Medium/Mediumship

In both Spiritism and Spiritualism, the physical and spiritual planes are bridged by people who are considered mediums. According to the dictionary, a *medium* is: "... an individual held to be a channel of communication between the earthly world and a world of spirits ..." Another definition of medium, found in the writing of Mary T. Longley of the National Spiritualist Association of Churches, says basically the same thing:

"A medium is one whose organism is sensitive to vibrations from the spirit world and through whose instrumentality, intelligences in that world are able to convey messages and produce the phenomena of Spiritualism. The office of mediumship is to bless humanity ..." (20)

These definitions express the idea that mediumship involves a cooperative effort between a person on the Earth plane and an entity existing on the spiritual plane. Mediumship in action is aptly portrayed in the popular television series *MEDIUM,* which is taken directly from the real life experiences of Allison DuBois, written about in her book *Don't Kiss Them Good-bye.* (21)

Continued on page 151.

The Most Revered Mayor of Baguio

Ang kapakumbabaan, haligi ng kabanalan.
Humility is the pillar of piety.

The narrow, twisting road winds up into the steep mountains north of Baguio. As the jeepney grinds its gears for the difficult climb, I try to prepare myself for a visit to one of the most famous psychic surgeons in the Philippines, Rev. Jun Labo, who is also the Mayor of Baguio. People come from all over the world for healing in his clinic at the Nagoya Inn.

After hearing about Jun Labo's amazing abilities, I am curious to find out if he can help me, because although I have been spiritually, mentally, and emotionally changed by my experiences with the faith healers, the doctor says I still have a fibroid.

I enter the front door of the Nagoya Inn, and am taken to a small chapel that smells strongly of incense. Intricately carved statutes of Jesus and Buddha grace the altar, and Buddhist chanting echoes from an adjoining room, marking a curious mix of cultures. The entire wall behind the altar is painted with an elaborate picture of what appears to be the Garden of Eden. In the center of the garden there is an eye within a triangle radiating light, symbolizing the Holy Spirit. After a few moments, I am led into a small office adjoining the chapel.

"Why have you come?" says the quiet, unassuming Jun Labo, who is sitting behind a simple wooden desk. "Do you come for healing?" He seems rather surprised that an American girl has arrived at his door unannounced and without the security of a guided tour or other companion.

147

"Yes," I reply, without looking directly at him.

We discuss the price, settling on the sum of $50 per day. This is much higher than the donations usually given at the churches in the rural areas, but lower than the fees charged by other healers at the hotels in Manila.

After this brief interview, I follow a series of signs marked only with arrows pointing down winding stairs leading to the basement. Soon I am in a large room filled with people of different ages, physical conditions, and nationalities: German, Indian, and Filipino, but mostly Japanese. They are all in various stages of undress, and many are covered with only a small, white towel, as they wait quietly in line for their turn on the two healing tables. *I had always thought the Japanese were modest, yet here was a large group of nearly-naked Japanese people.*

A sign on the wall says: "Please Fall in Line," meaning "Please Form a Line." This terminology is likely left over from the long occupation of the Philippines by the American military. But there is a certain irony to it, because some of the people in this particular line do, in fact, look as if they might fall over at any moment.

After undressing and leaving my clothes in a tidy pile, I wrap as much of my body as possible with a towel and take my place with the others. While waiting, I observe the incredible events unfolding about eight feet away.

Jun Labo's Japanese wife, Yuko, is in a state of deep concentration as she performs psychic surgery on the stream of people who quickly move on and off the table in front of her. Many of the tumors she removes are as large as grapefruit. She looks like an angel. She seems to float in the air a few inches above the floor.

I observe as a middle-aged man gets on the table and lies face down. Yuko first washes her hands, and after asking her assistant to spread the man's buttocks apart, she begins to dig her fingers into his rectum. I watch in amazement as she pulls out a clump of stringy, white tissue and drops it into a bucket on the floor. The room is momentarily brightened by the flashing light of a camera. The waiting crowd leans forward *en masse* and lets out a simultaneous groan of relief. The experience of the man on the table has mirrored everyone's personal expectations.

Jun Labo quietly enters the clinic with several assistants, bows his head in prayer for a few moments, and begins to work on someone lying on another table. A beatific look of grace appears on his face as the Holy Spirit comes over him. I am hardly able to remain upright because the energy in the room has become so intense with his presence. I tremble and my breath begins to quicken.

When I reach the head of the line, I hand my camera to the man standing behind me and ask him to take photographs of my surgery. Lying down on the hard, wooden table before Jun Labo, he begins to remove large blood clots and stringy tissue from my lower abdomen. There is no pain, only tugging and that same feeling of floating I have experienced during healing with other psychic surgeons.

His assistant tells me to get off the table and move to Yuko's table. She also presses her hands into my stomach. I am able to lift my head slightly and see her remove several growths about the size of an orange. She holds each one up above me and looks at it with concern, her eyes half-closed. Even she seems amazed at what is happening.

A wave of gratitude and peace washes over me as I return to the sidelines and watch growths of all sizes and shapes being removed from other people. Some of my fellow seekers cover their noses delicately with their handkerchiefs to block out the smell of blood and disease that has begun to fill the room.

A Japanese man in his 20s or 30s, who looked like he was in the final stages of cancer, was carried in on a stretcher the first day I was at the clinic. He was terribly thin and weak. They laid him gently on Yuko's table, and when she removed an enormous tumor from his abdomen, about the size of a small watermelon, everyone in the room gasped in amazement. He was carried in again on the second and third days.

But on the fourth day, when he walked in completely unassisted, a gentle and hopeful smile on his face, I thought: *Did not Lazarus arise from the dead on the fourth day? And did not Christ himself also arise from the dead?* (22 John 1-44)

∘−◁▩▷−∘

Skeptics have averred that the tissues removed during psychic surgery are actually chicken guts or other animal parts that have been hidden inside the sleeves of the healers. At the Nagoya Inn, however, the things I observed being removed were too big to be hidden, and Jun and Yuko Labo wore clothing with short sleeves. Not only did I observe dozens of tumors being removed—from a distance of about six feet away—I also heard them hit the bottom of the bucket with a resounding thud when they were discarded. This is experience that cannot be easily dismissed or refuted.

∘−◁▩▷−∘

Afterwards, while waiting for the jeepney, I felt as though my body had been turned inside out. Although I was physically exhausted, as might be expected after receiving any kind of surgery, my faith had been renewed. My understanding of the nature of reality was shifted when these two healers blessed me with the Grace of God, which fell from their hands like sparkling waterfalls, crystal clear diamonds.

The Miracle
and the Enigma

The gift of mediumship can be given by Holy Spirit, but a medium must also endeavor to develop spiritual consciousness. Mediums perform a wide variety of functions in addition to healing, including prophecy. Mediums have different abilities, including: sensitives (who feel the presence of spirits), clairvoyants (who see spirits), clairaudients (who hear spirits), materialization of solid matter from the spirit plane, and automatic writing.

In the Filipino Spiritist churches, mediums go into trance for the singular purpose of allowing the Holy Spirit to enter and work through them. They transmit verbal teachings channeled from Spirit, assign Bible studies, perform magnetic healing and psychic surgery, and counsel people who are experiencing personal difficulties.

In the words of John of God: "To be a medium requires loving God above all else. Love your fellow beings as yourself. It is necessary to have a deep faith in a Higher Power." (11)

Continued on page 159.

Mely's Prophecy

◦◦◦◦◦✳◦◦◦◦◦

An gaong magagadanon, Totoo an tataramon.
A dying man's words can never lie.

During the Sunday church service on the last weekend of my visit, I gave a short sermon in English on the subject of forgiveness, hoping they would understand at least some of it. Afterwards, Belen was inducted into the trance state and began to speak as the medium, while scribbling on a piece of paper.

Unexpectedly, after a few minutes she called me back to the front of the room. Standing before her, I became aware of a bright beam of light coming from the center of her forehead and entering into the center of my forehead. Although my eyes were closed, I could see this clairvoyantly with my inner vision. I understood this experience to mean the Holy Spirit was opening my third eye—located within the sixth chakra, which is in the area between the physical eyes. This *opening* meant my ability to see the non-material reality of other dimensions was being strengthened—like wiping dirt from a mirror or window in order to see more clearly.

Next, my head was spontaneously lowered in slow motion by some unknown force, as if someone or something was pushing it towards the floor. From this position, the light entered the top of my head, which is known as the *crown*, or seventh, chakra. Some people say awakening of the crown chakra can lead to god-realization or realization of the self—a state of total spiritual illumination and understanding.

"Now is the time for you to receive more *power*," said the medium.

◦◦◦◦◦✳◦◦◦◦◦

When used in this context, the word "power" refers to spiritual power, meaning the ability to channel stronger energy for healing.

I held my hands open in front of her, and she performed the now-familiar ritual of pouring energy into my palms for a few minutes and then pressing them together. Afterwards, I felt as if my hands were no longer attached to the rest of my body. I began to shake. All desire to touch or grasp was gone. The feeling was one of pure magic, total joy. The top of my head and my forehead were tingling and buzzing with energy when I returned to my seat.

Towards the end of the service, I was called to the front again to receive my official certificate of ordination as a Minister and Healer of the Faith In God Spiritual Church:

TO ALL WHOM THESE GREETINGS MAY COME:

Know ye people of our Lord God that Jessica C. Bryan, having proven worthy, and in recognition hereof is ordained as MINISTER (HONORARY) in accordance with the usages of this church; and by reason and will of the Holy Spirit, she is likewise authorized to preach the gospel of Jesus Christ, to perform spiritual healing by the laying on of the hands with prayer and faith, as long as her manner of life and conversation is perpetually becoming in abiding principles to the ethical doctrines of the church.

IN TESTIMONY WHEREOF, I hereunto set my hand and cause the seal of the church to be affixed this 19th day of January, in the Year of our Lord nineteen hundred and ninety-five.

ATTESTED: Estifanio M. Banao, Secretary General
Rev. Juliana N. Onia, Bishop

After the service, a group of us went next door for lunch and fellowship, and to be with Mely. I was sitting next to her when she unexpectedly opened her eyes, fixed me in her gaze, and whispered—with a room full of people as witnesses:

"If I should die . . . and you should be the medium . . . then I will speak through you . . . and that will be the proof."

153

The Reluctant Healer

Back in Berkeley

Mapipia anusumavat ka a maysaosaod su,
sagap as canu caviden mu du calawangan, a manalamad su among.
It is better to go home and weave a net than stay
in the beach and watch the fishes.

I left the Philippines not long after Mely's mysterious prophecy at Christmas, and the culture shock of Berkeley was far worse than that of Manila. During my first trip to the grocery store, I was run into by more than one frantic woman pushing a cart piled high with food. Driving was even worse. I avoided it as much as possible for the first week.

Everything and everyone was moving so fast I could not keep up. My "inner clock" had been altered, my circadian rhythms changed. I had become Filipino in my relationship to time and action, which is expressed in the phrase "by and by." This means everything happens at the right moment, even if you have to wait a very long time for the moment to arrive.

Life in the Philippines is relaxed and often free of expectations, so whatever happens is a delightful surprise. I longed for that feeling of living moment to moment and falling into the rhythm of daily life with relaxed breath. But, slowly, things returned to "normal," and I went back to work as a legal secretary.

In March, I received a letter from Belen saying Mely had passed away. It all seemed so sad and far away. Mely had been so different at Christmas, compared to when I had first met her. I hardly recognized her as the same person. It felt like the Mely who had just died was a stranger. Even before her actual death, it seemed like she had shifted her consciousness to somewhere else. She had already moved on. Now, the first part of her prophecy, so casually given, had become a reality.

One Saturday night the following August, I was sleeping over at Dottie's house in Davis. Ralph, an ordained minister from the Berkeley Psychic Institute, was with us. We were planning to drive to Connie's church in Lemmon Valley the next day.

Dottie had been studying Reiki, a gentle, hands-on method of channeling universal energy to reduce stress and promote health; Ralph was a psychic who receives messages from Spirit; and I was trying to understand what being a medium meant.

We decided to play with different spiritual techniques. Dottie lay down on the floor with her eyes closed, and my hands began to flutter in the air around her. I felt slightly dizzy, but I was trying to follow the energy as it moved through me and into her. Ralph sat nearby, also with his eyes closed.

"What do you see? What am I doing?" I asked him.

A hearty laugh came from deep in his belly. "Oh yes. Mely is here in spirit. She is sitting directly behind you. She is attached to your hand chakras by cords of blue light. She is showing you where and how to place your hands. She is laughing and laughing. Oh what a happy spirit."

"Can I talk to her? Can I ask a question?"

"Yes, of course."

Hoping Mely could hear me, I asked my most pressing question, "What is it like to be dead?"

Ralph, speaking as Mely, responded: "At first, I missed my family and friends, and especially my dog, but now I'm quite used to it. Best of all, I don't have to do my hair in the morning anymore."

We all laughed, because this kind of humor was so typical of her when she was alive. We knew that we had really spoken with the spirit of Filomena Naces.

The Miracle
and the Enigma

Discarnate beings can take different forms, and may be called by different names, depending on the context in which a particular spirit communicates. In some settings, channeled spirits are referred to as *out-of-body entities* or *spirit guides*. A fascinating example is found in the case of Arigo, the "Surgeon of the Rusty Knife." (22) This simple man, with no medical training, had a spirit guide who was believed to be a deceased German physician named "Dr. Fritz." Arigo's guide instructed him in performing hundreds of successful "operations" using only a rusty knife.

Spirit guides enter the mind and body of a healer, while the healer is in a full trance, and make use of their physical facilities to administer curative power. The spirit may send thought impressions to the healer giving instructions. Spirit guides are often the spirits of eminent doctors or saints who have passed over. They become spirit guides in order to continue the good deeds they started while on Earth. John of God is a particularly powerful example of this phenomenon, because he channels over thirty "spirit doctors" when he performs psychic surgery.

Another example of mediumship is Jonathan Edwards, the television psychic, who acts as an intermediary between dead people and their living relatives in the studio audience.

Continued on page 164.

The Reluctant Healer

A na abe, mag-guibo man bagana ulod.
He who is reluctant moves like an earthworm.

At the time of my trips to the Philippines in the early 1990s, I had never heard the term "medical intuitive," although I knew about Edgar Cayce, "The Sleeping Prophet," who diagnosed disease and offered treatment suggestions while he was unconscious. I only knew that I could "see" inside the body: dark, stagnant energy forms, swarming, wiggling things, thickenings colored deep blue and black. It was fascinating, but also frightening. I did not understand what was expected of me. Nevertheless, I bought a massage table, told everyone I knew that I needed people to "practice on," and began to explore the experience.

My attention was drawn to dark areas in the [etheric] body. This told me where to put my hands. Sometimes, I heard an authoritative voice coming out of nowhere that gave instructions. I might see something on the "television screen" in the middle of my head that would give me information about the person's concerns or health issues. It was like looking at a clear pane of glass where pictures and words would form. Mely's prophecy: ". . . and you should be the medium" was starting to make sense.

A casual acquaintance, Billie, was the first person to make an appointment. He had trouble with his lungs. When Billie lay down on the table on his back, I could see his lungs, even though my eyes were closed. They were almost black and hardly moving. His chest seemed frozen.

My hands began to emit a strange vibration that seemed almost electrical, and, somehow, I knew exactly what to do. I put my hand inside his chest—my etheric hand, not my physical hand—and grasping one lung firmly, I squeezed it as hard as I could. My entire body became hot and I began to sweat. After a few minutes, perhaps less, I felt a feeble pulse in the lung. Giving one final squeeze, I let go and pulled back my hand. Now, the lung was pulsing deeply and rhythmically, and it was a healthy red. I did the same thing with the other lung, and again there was the same response.

I opened my eyes and looked at Billie lying on the table, his chest rising and falling gracefully. What happened? I struggled to understand it.

He asked what I had seen and done. When I told him, he stared at me for a moment as if he did not believe me. Then he blanched white and said, "The doctor told me to stop smoking crack cocaine or I would be dead within five years."

Billie got up from the table and practically ran from the room. He seemed unable to acknowledge the positive effects of his healing. He saw only the dark and stagnant, remembered only the dire pronouncement of the medical doctor.

I saw him about three months later at a party. "How is your lung condition?" I said.

"My asthma is completely gone. The air pollution count must be down in San Francisco because I haven't had an attack in several months."

This told me that Billie's healing had "worked." However, it seemed like he had repressed all memory of it. He was unable to move out of the old paradigm and into a new, spiritually-expanded belief system. From his objective point of view, he had lain down on a massage table and after a half hour of being touched gently by a woman he hardly knew, he had gotten up and gone home. In Billie's mind it was easier to attribute his newfound health to a change in air quality than to admit that he had been touched by Divine energy.

My experience with Billie taught me to use discrimination in deciding what to say. The person receiving healing may not be ready to hear the entire truth. I was discouraged, but I also knew I had to give up the need for validation. Healing might not come in a form that can be recognized; it might not be acknowledged at all; or it might even be denied outright. Healing belongs to the one receiving it—the medium merely delivers the message.

∞◦═◆═◦∞

A woman with severe mental and emotional problems came to see me. She started crying and could not stop for almost three hours. She claimed I had somehow altered her homeopathic remedy, and that her problems were all my "fault."

Many people have the tendency to blame others for their difficulties, which can prevent them from attaining inner peace and good health. When we look outside of ourselves for a "cure," we are unable to find our own solutions. As a potential healer, I needed to be strong, objective, and stand firm in my own integrity. I also knew I needed to set boundaries so others could not "move into my space" and stay there. This includes creating boundaries on the etheric level to avoid becoming filled with the negative psychic energy of other people.

∞◦═◆═◦∞

I went to a drumming circle in Marin County. They were having a memorial session dedicated to someone who was in the hospital dying from cancer. I had never met the man, but after the drumming was over, I picked up his photograph from an altar in the center of the circle.

Looking at the photo, I went into a deep trance and saw immediately how the cancer had started in his colon and from there metastasized to his liver and throughout his body. He was obviously dying. Horrified, I ran from the room and almost threw up in the parking lot. It frightened me. I felt like I had somehow "caught" the man's illness.

Becoming a medium is a serious endeavor that must be entered into with care. The rule "Do No Harm" applies to everyone involved, including the medium. Clearly, I needed to learn more about how to protect myself. How could I help others if I was reluctant to touch them for fear of "catching" their illness?

I met a man who taught a class in psychic awareness. He was ill with some undiagnosed illness and weighed only 110 pounds. All he could eat was thoroughly cooked white rice and occasionally a banana. After several healing sessions, I saw something moving independently in the area of his liver, and I realized he had some kind of worms or parasites. When I told him, his eyes flew open and he looked at me with fear.

"*Now*, I know what you're doing," he said.

He was psychic, after all, so I expected him to *know*. I wanted him to explain it to me. I certainly did not expect him to become frightened and leave, and never return. I can only hope he went for the appropriate medical treatment and is now thriving.

Magnetic healing and clairvoyance are incredibly helpful diagnostic tools that can be used in conjunction with more conventional treatment, but unfortunately, these methods can also be frightening because they are so far from normal, rational experience, even to people who are familiar with metaphysics.

Spirit had landed me in a big dilemma. I needed ongoing support in my development as a healer, but the church in the Philippines was 16,000 miles away. Connie occasionally offered advice, but she was usually too busy running the church in Nevada.

Around this time, I consulted a telephone psychic who had a good reputation. She specialized in working with difficult illnesses such as AIDS. When I told her about my experiences, I heard her sharp intake of breath.

"You're channeling alien entities from the Fifth Universe over," she said. "STOP IMMEDIATELY. IT'S TOO DANGEROUS."

I had no idea what she was talking about. *Alien entities? The Fifth Universe over? Over where?*

But although her meaning was unclear, the panic in her voice was evident. So, I took her advice. I sold the massage table and stopped trying to be a healer, or even thinking about it. Of course, later I realized she was only mirroring my own fear back to me.

The Miracle
and the Enigma

Out-of-body entities can also have non-benevolent purposes. They may be called by names such as *nature spirit* or *demon,* indicating a negative spirit of low evolution with a destructive or selfish purpose. Under certain conditions, earthbound entities can possess a person, causing ill health and troubled emotional states. This type of spirit attachment is not possible if a person's energy field is healthy and strong, but if the field is weakened by illness, drugs, accidents, or a negative attitude, an opening is created. In these cases, an exorcism of the possessing entity may be necessary.

Most healers start out with lofty goals and a pure desire to benefit their fellow humans, but they can fall prey to the desire for power and material benefit. This type of spiritual corruption is believed to make it possible for a medium to channel destructive entities. Purity of purpose can be difficult for a healer to master and maintain.

Mediumship should be avoided during physical illness. Mediums should have good morals and conduct, and be free of mental and emotional problems. Care must be taken to get enough rest in order to restore energy and balance, and a healthy diet should be followed. Mediums must always endeavor to live a peaceful life in order to preserve their health, and to avoid becoming a channel for destructive spirits.

Eight Years Later

∘•⊶❋⊷•∘

Aanhin pa ang bagong ilawan, kung hindi rin sisindihan.
What good is a new lamp if it will not be lighted?

In 2004, eight years later, I was living near the Oregon Coast with my partner, who is a chiropractor. During the eight years since I had been to the Philippines, I had not done magnetic healing, although I sometimes felt guilty about ignoring this gift from the Holy Spirit.

We went to Eugene for the Saturday Market, and I noticed a sign on a sidewalk booth that read: "Psychic Readings Channeled from Pleiades: $20." It reminded me of Connie, and the woman looked harmless enough, so I sat down in the chair across from her.

"What concerns you?" she said.

"I am filled with remorse because I was given the gift of spiritual healing, but I have not honored it because I'm afraid."

"How can I help you?"

"I need to speak with Filomena Naces, a healer who has passed over. I was initiated at her church in the Philippines."

The woman nodded her head "Yes," and went into a light trance.

"Tell Mely I'm sorry so many years have passed and I still haven't pursued magnetic healing."

"Yes, I have her here. She's laughing. She says, 'It doesn't matter, because here there is no time. Trust what you've been given.' She indicates that she will help you when you're ready."

Soon after this meeting with the psychic in Eugene, I was ready. When I was able to set aside my skeptical mind and became a willing instrument, things began to happen. To be a healer one must be receptive and have faith in God. It is not that I was looking for it, but rather I overcame my fear and allowed the process to unfold. My spiritual understanding had matured.

The opportunity to work with another healer, Alicia, presented itself. She invited a woman who was severely depressed to come to us for healing—I'll call the woman Mary. The three of us met at my partner's chiropractic office for the session.

Mary's sadness was quite apparent when she came into the treatment room. Her shoulders were slumped and her complexion ashen. She looked to be about fifty years old and was extremely overweight. Strangely, all the extra weight was in her stomach. It was enormous. Although she was not pregnant, she looked like she was about to give birth.

She lay on the table on her back, with Alicia at her feet and me at her side. We went into trance, and Alicia began to run energy into the soles of Mary's feet and up through her body.

I sat there for a moment, until I became aware of a tiny spirit baby attached by a cord of golden light to Mary's abdomen. The baby saw me looking at it and became agitated, as if it was upset that it had been discovered. I had the definite impression that this being was in hiding.

Psychic "cords" are telepathic, energy links between people. They can be temporary or last a long time. Many people do not even know they have them. Cords can represent positive connections between two individuals, but they can also be harmful in situations where one person drains another of vitality. They can be removed by a psychic practitioner, or you can remove them yourself by swimming in the ocean or taking a bath with sea salt or lavender. Surrounding yourself with white light energy can be especially helpful in preventing cord attachments. There are also many ways of visualizing the cords in meditation and dissolving them.

I told Mary what I saw, and asked if she had ever had a miscarriage, thinking the baby was the spirit of a child who had lost its body and was confused. Souls in this situation are called *earthbounds* because they do not realize their body has died. They are unaware that they are supposed to go to the *light*, a higher plane of existence some people call *heaven*.

When Mary indicated that she had never been pregnant, nor had she given birth to a living child, Alicia and I just looked at each other. We could not understand why this spirit baby was attached to Mary.

But then Mary provided the answer: "When my mother was pregnant, I had a twin, but my twin died at birth."

Suddenly, it became obvious that the child attached to Mary by the golden energy cord was, in fact, her twin, who thought it was still in utero. It was waiting to be born, to receive the body it expected. A shiver went through me, and the hair on my arms stood up as if electrified.

"The spirit baby is the soul of your twin," I told Mary. "Do you want me to detach it and send it to the light?

"Yes, of course, if you can," she said.

I wrapped my [etheric] hand firmly around the cord close to where it was attached and began to pull. I was surprised at its depth—it seemed to go all the way through her body to her backbone. At the superficial level of attachment the cord became thicker and spread across about six inches of Mary's abdomen.

I pulled and pulled, but it was surprisingly difficult to move. I spontaneously began to breathe heavy—the bellows breathing called *pranayama* by those who practice yoga. The energy in the room became tense as the baby soul frantically flew about at the other end of the cord, desperately trying to hold onto Mary.

After about three minutes, although it seemed much longer, the cord broke away with a snap so loud that I could almost hear it with my physical ears. In one instant, less than a second, an interdimensional door opened over the table up near the ceiling and a brilliant light appeared. The baby being and the cord instantly flew into the opening and the door slammed shut behind them.

For a few minutes, we were quiet and filled with peace. We were reverent at the miracle of this "birth," which was also a "death." We honored the soul of Mary's dead twin, now on its way to God.

Mary appeared changed when she got up from the table. I couldn't believe it. She looked like a different person than the one who had walked into the room, depressed and hunched over. She began to cry tears of joy and relief, and then left with a broad grin on her face.

About a year later, I received a phone call from Alicia. She had seen Mary, and wanted me to know that Mary had lost about fifty pounds—all the extra weight she had been carrying for years. Alicia said Mary was completely healthy and vibrant.

Sometimes, when people ask me what I am going to do during a healing session I tell them, "Heck if I know." Truly, I never know what to expect, as Mary's story so aptly illustrates. I am usually as surprised as the person on the table—because I am *not* doing the healing, but rather functioning as a conduit for a Higher Power.

∘∘◁▭⫛▭▷∘∘

I began to struggle with finding a more defined space in my life for my work as a healer. Should I open an office? Start a church? Put up flyers? Rent a booth at a psychic fair? Nothing seemed right. Finally, I surrendered and prayed to God: "If you want me to be a healer, you will have to bring people to my front door, because I cannot do it on my own."

Two days later, a man came to see us because his wife, Susan, had fallen out of the back door while intoxicated at nine in the morning. Her neck was badly injured and she was paralyzed. My partner was hesitant to intervene with chiropractic care because of legal and medical issues, but the husband of the injured woman was open to spiritual healing.

Several weeks later, when she was moved from the hospital to a rehabilitation center, I visited her for the first time. The situation was tragic. Susan lay in bed, unable to move her body except her head and arms. Even with pain medication, she was in severe pain from the injury.

After a brief introduction, I stood at the head of the bed, closed my eyes, and began to say the Lord's Prayer out loud, with Susan joining in. Susan and her husband were Christians and, in the metaphysical sense, the seventh chakra at the top of the head opens with the recitation of this prayer.

Guided by spirit, I put my hands first above and then lightly touching the top of Susan's head. Then I did something called "spinning the chakras." This is like unscrewing the lid off a jar—my hand makes a twirling motion. Almost immediately, a flood of negative feelings exploded out of the top of her head.

There was grief, fear, anger, and frustration—I felt her emotions in my own body as she released them. I became dizzy and had to grab the side of the hospital bed to remain upright. After several minutes, Susan's emotional eruption began to subside, and sensing the healing was complete, I removed my hands. Susan opened her eyes and burst into hysterical weeping. Her husband was watching, and it upset him to see her crying.

After about five minutes, she sputtered down to a steady sob and then became quiet. She looked at me with crystal clarity in her eyes. "How can I ever thank you," she said. "This is the first time I have been able to cry in the three months since my accident. What a relief."

This was a powerful experience for both of us—to think that she had been lying there for three months and had not been able to cry. I was very happy with the results of the session.

The next time I saw her, Susan complained about her hands being drawn up like claws. She could not hold a fork to feed herself. I went into trance and concentrated on running energy into her body through the top of her head, passing golden light into the injured area of her neck and spine, and then down her arms and into her hands.

She started to get "electrical shocks" moving through her torso and legs. It was the first time she had felt much of anything in her lower body since the accident, and she seemed encouraged by the feelings, even though they were uncomfortable. I thought of it as her nerves "coming back on-line."

We continued this type treatment for several sessions, and as the electrical sensations became stronger they gradually became less painful. After these treatments, Susan's ability to feed herself started to improve, although she still had trouble getting soup to her mouth without spilling it. She also started to get back some strength in her legs and was more able to participate in physical therapy.

At one point, I visualized Susan's injury in my meditation the night before I was scheduled to see her. I observed massive bruising and swelling, and several vertebrae were pushed to one side. The spinal cord had been damaged, but it had not been severed. I did long-distance healing and applied what I call a *psychic bandage:* a patch of white light energy that provides ongoing benefit.

When I told the physical therapist what I had seen, he was amazed. He told me I had described the exact nature of her injury, as shown on the MRI. In terms of *my* experience, this was a miracle. There are many medical intuitives who can have been trained to "read" the body, but I never expected this kind of information would come through me.

Susan's story has a sad ending. Her husband consulted a surgeon, and it was decided that surgery on the initial injury might alleviate her condition. Surgery was performed, actually several surgeries, but unfortunately to no avail.

Afterwards, Susan was so disoriented because of pain, medication, and surgical trauma that I was no longer able to work with her. It was just too difficult for both of us.

Why did Susan fall out the back door? Why was she drinking beer at nine in the morning? The answers to these and other questions about this case might be found in an understanding of Susan's karma, specifically her relationship with her husband and her son, who died at a young age. She told me she had never been treated with as much kindness as she had received after her injury. Perhaps she had always longed for someone to take care of her. Maybe her illness represented her unresolved grief over losing a child. Perhaps there is no reason at all, and falling out the back door was merely a cruel twist of fate.

From Susan, I learned to be careful about getting emotionally attached. I had great compassion for her, and this made it hard to be objective. I *needed* her to walk again. I also learned there may be reasons for illness that serve a purpose I will never understand.

⊶⊸❈⊷⊶

Healing sometimes helps caregivers more than the person who is sick, especially in cases where someone is dying. In this way, the ill person is helped indirectly. I visited a woman in the hospital who was paralyzed after a heart attack she had suffered during childbirth—I'll call her Maggie. The family believed she was "still in there," but they needed reassurance.

Maggie's mother was obviously devoted to her care. Maggie had been in the hospital for about four years, and her room looked much like a regular bedroom at home. The walls were covered with photographs of her children, and there were stuffed animals and other mementos.

Maggie's mother hovered around her, patting her constantly, and doing whatever she could for Maggie's comfort. She gave me the case history and recounted that the week before Maggie had started yelling during a visit from her estranged husband, even with the tracheotomy tube in her throat.

When I stood close to Maggie and introduced myself, she turned her head and looked directly at me. Her eyes were piercing. They communicated her frustration, her rage at her husband for abandoning her, and her desire to be with her children. She was really THERE, even more so than if she had actually spoken out loud. Maggie wanted to communicate and move her body, but her condition prevented it.

I stood behind her and put my hands above her head. When I began to go into trance, Maggie jerked her head before I even touched her. At this point, her mother exclaimed, "She felt that!"

Almost immediately, I saw the brain injury in the upper left part of her head. It was a light shade of grey, with thin, hair-like, white lines running through it. Maggie's body was obviously engaged in the slow process of dissolving a blood clot or some other debris.

This healing session was quite short, only about five minutes. Because of Maggie's sensitive condition, I was wary of overdoing it. I placed a psychic bandage on the injured area and removed my hands.

Mary's mother became visibly excited when I told her what I had seen. "That's exactly what the brain injury researcher from Stanford said. I know Maggie is still conscious, she just can't express herself."

As we walked to the physical therapy facility, pushing Maggie in her wheelchair, her mother continued to talk about how relieved she was to hear my opinion that Maggie was fighting hard to recover. Maggie's mother already knew this, but to hear it from a spiritual healer was reassuring. I had given her renewed hope. She said, "I'm seventy years old now, and I come to the hospital every day, all day, so hope is a very good thing."

When I left, Maggie's mother was strapping Maggie's inert legs into an elaborate machine designed to move her legs for her as if she were riding a bike. Maggie's mother is determined that when her daughter's brain recovers, her body will still be functional.

I do not know if the energy healing I facilitated for Maggie will help her. Likely, she needs this kind of work on a regular basis, but unfortunately she is in a facility located 300 miles from where I live. It is clear that strengthening the faith of her mother, who takes care of her every day, will also help Maggie.

◦◦◦◆◦◦◦

On a lighter note, Vicky came to see me because she was having trouble getting over her anger at her former husband. They had been divorced five years previously and he was remarried. They had been together for about twenty-five years and had two children. Vicky also complained of feeling exhausted and not being able to run her business effectively. She felt that after five years, "enough was enough."

As she relaxed into the table, I rested my hands lightly on her arm. My inner vision began to come into focus, and I saw an energetic cord plugged into her third chakra (in the area of her belly button). Much to my surprise, on the other end of the cord was the energy of Vicky's former husband. Even though he was remarried, he was still *feeding* off Vicky's vitality like a nursing infant. This must have been a pattern in their relationship, and he had not let go of it. No wonder Vicky felt exhausted. She was giving herself away without even knowing it.

I told her what I saw, and, of course, she was as surprised as I was. She had mistakenly thought the problem rested with her, that *she* was the one who could not let go of *him*.

I asked her if she wanted me to remove the cord, and Vicky immediately yelled, "Take it out RIGHT NOW."

This cord was fairly easy to remove from Vicky's etheric body because she pushed it out as I pulled. The husband seemed surprised by what we were doing. Perhaps he, too, did not know he was still "plugged in" to Vicky. (During a clairvoyant reading or healing, an attached spirit emits an emotional, energetic pulse that can be perceived by the person doing the reading.)

At the end of the session, I told her that anytime she felt tired or upset, or even slightly negative, it might mean he was trying to reattach the cord. I advised her to create an energy shield around her body to prevent this. I told her to imagine it to be whatever felt right to her. She was still alarmed, but she was also relieved.

Vicky came back to see me about a month later. She said she was feeling great and had all her energy back, but she wanted to make sure that darn cord was not there again.

When she lay down on the table, I burst out laughing because Vicky had created an incredible shield. It was about three feet square, bright orange, and several inches thick. It looked like jousting armor from the Middle Ages. No one was going to penetrate this shield and abuse her psychically.

Over time, Vicky has eased up on creating her shield. Eventually, she will not need it anymore—unless, of course, someone else comes along and tries to take advantage of her.

Magnetic Healing

⋄−⊏⊐⋇⊏⊐−⋄

Irutam a petpetan ta sursuro, ta isu ti biagmo.
Grasp tightly what you have learned, for it is your life.

Since I first went to the Philippines in 1993, I have learned much about the Filipino healing art known as *magnetic healing*. Obviously, this is not healing with actual magnets, which has enjoyed a resurgence of popularity in recent years. Rather, in the "magnetic" sense, it is a method of pulling negative energy out of the body by manipulating the electromagnetic force fields that hold the body in solid form—we are not really solid in the Third Dimension, we only think we are. Disease begins in the etheric body, and by the time the physical body has become ill, the problem has been going on for a long time. Conversely, as we heal on the etheric, so do we heal the physical, but sometimes it takes awhile or it might not happen at all.

Magnetic healing creates an internal physical environment that enables people to heal themselves, to self-correct. The word *healing* comes from the Middle English word *haelin*, meaning "to make whole." Magnetic healing is similar to the practice of *laying on of hands* and many other types of energy healing. One of the more interesting is found in Native American traditions:

Ronnie Tallman of the Navajo Nation was surprised when he realized he was able to diagnose illness. He was eventually sanctified as a *hand trembler* in a ceremony conducted by his uncle and grandfather, and he became a certified medicine man. Ronnie describes an experience nearly identical to what I have felt during magnetic healing:

"My left hand started to shake, and at the same time, an amazing feeling of calmness came over me. My heart slowed down and I felt

174

peaceful. My hand kept trembling, and I started to notice the energy in the people around me, and I started to know things about them that I could never have known, things about their lives and what made them sick or in pain." (23)

∘∘⊏⊏✳⊐⊐∘∘

Magnetic healing is spontaneous and requires total detachment from the material world or any form of engagement with a worldly method. It seems guided by a thinking intelligence, and although the current seems to focus on the target areas, it also seems to possess an automatic switch-off mechanism. When a healing session is complete, the magnetic current—which is usually felt as heat and vibration—begins to gradually diminish until it disappears completely.

Positive results are more likely to occur when there is an affinity between the healer and the spirit doctors working through the healer, as well as an affinity between the healer and the person receiving healing.

Magnetic healing is the most common method of healing used by the Filipino faith healers, and as with psychic surgery, it occurs while the healer is in a trance state and functioning as a medium. In addition to removing negative energy, a magnetic healer also channels the Divine energy of God into those who are suffering. This flow of energy can occur in different ways.

Sometimes the magnetic healer touches the body; sometimes only the etheric body is touched.

This manifests as the healer stroking the air a few inches away from the patient's body.

A procedure called a *spiritual injection* may be used. In this case, energy flows out of the healer's pointed index finger and into another person in a rather forceful burst of energy, much like an actual injection. Spinning the chakras, as previously discussed, is another way of manipulating the etheric body to facilitate healing.

Magnetic healing is sometimes said to be a precursor to the ability to perform psychic surgery. As the magnetic healer gains in faith and "the power," it is believed that she can move from the ability to pull the *energy* of diseased tissue out of the body, to being able to remove the physical manifestation of disease.

In both magnetic healing and psychic surgery there is a strong emphasis on the idea that the human medium does not do the healing, but rather the Holy Spirit is given credit for any benefit received. Healing happens by Divine Will, according to the particular situation and the intention of the participants.

Expectations

Nung pangatawanan, alang e agawa
If you exert all your effort, nothing is impossible.

A visit to a psychic surgeon or faith healer might not always meet expectations, including the elimination of physical illness, but it can bring about healing of the mind, emotions, or spirit, resulting in a dramatic change in the way a person views his or her life situation.

In her book *How People Heal* (24), Diane Goldner writes:

> "Healing really is not about curing. Even if the emotional and spiritual levels are healed, the body does not always have time to catch up."

She goes on to quote healer and teacher Rosalyn Bruyere (25):

> "If you do the work you might still die anyway. Sometimes a situation has gone too long with too many components to be easily healed. Spirituality is not going to save us. That idea is left over from early views of religion. The point of religion is living well, not saving yourself."

According to spiritual teacher, healer, clairvoyant, and author of *YOU ARE THE ANSWER*, Michael J. Tamura:

> "Healing isn't just about recovering from an illness or injury. True healing is restoring one's self to wholeness. It is our homecoming to Spirit and Divinity. And with every step we take in this healing journey we move closer to the fulfillment of our soul purpose.
>
> "The restoring of our faith and certainty in Spirit is the greatest healing gift offered through 'psychic surgery.' The master healer Jesus himself taught that it is our faith that heals us. Thus, when we place ourselves in the presence of a healer

who has complete faith in the All-Forgiving, we regain our certainty that we are Spirit. Any invalidating and limiting beliefs we have long-held within us begin to dissolve. These hidden beliefs also include self-limiting concepts from others that we have adopted. Illness results if we hold on to self-destructive concepts within us long enough.

"If you are preparing to receive faith healing and psychic surgery, clarify for yourself what you are truly asking for in the healing, and have certainty in the truth, love, and goodness of Divine Spirit. Then, the healers will bring the Light of Oneness directly to any divisive energy such as blame, doubt, judgment, or anger that you have unconsciously held against yourself. Be aware as the real miracles begin to unfold when you let go of invalidating yourself. Psychic surgery can be one of the finest forms of preventative (spiritual) medicine." (26)

Caroline Myss says in her book *Why People Don't Heal and How They Can*:

"Healing and change are one and the same thing. They are composed of the same energy, and we cannot seek to heal an illness without first looking into what behavioral patterns and attitudes need to be altered in our life. Once those characteristics are identified, we have to do something about those patterns. This requires taking action, and action brings about change." (27)

The ultimate purpose of faith healing is to help a person become aware of their own spiritual nature, and to help them lead a life based on spiritual values. When a person who has been declared "hopeless" by medical science is helped by psychic or spiritual healing, he invariably alters his way of life to embrace higher standards and spiritual values.

Heather Cumming writes in *John of God: The Brazilian Healer Who's Touched the Lives of Millions*:

"Occasionally, people come to the Casa in the final stages of an illness. Their organs are too depleted to hold the energy of a physical healing. This is not a failure, nor should it be seen as a judgment on the individual's willingness or ability to receive healing. Healing also takes place on the spiritual and karmic levels, and the soul often receives great support in preparing for transition. Many family members who have lost a loved one after visiting John of God have shared the person's feelings of serenity and equanimity, and explained how the entire family shared in this healing." (11)

◦◦⊂⊱✳⊰⊃◦◦

Psychic surgery and faith healing are best described in the extraordinary words of Rev. Alex Orbito:

"The entire healing process occurs in a different dimension. It is no miracle or magic. I just happen to be the medium through which God channels His divine energy.

"As I see the crowd of sick people waiting for me to relieve them of their suffering, my heart is filled with love, mercy, and compassion.

"I deeply concentrate and fervently pray to God to make me a channel of His healing power. I then utter a secret power word which was given to me by my master, or spirit guide, and all of a sudden, I am transformed into another being, a holy man, whose only remaining thought and feeling is one of love, mercy, and compassion towards the sick. At that moment, I no longer think of myself as Alex Orbito, but as a mere channel of God's healing energy.

"When this happens, I first feel a strange coldness all over my body as the spirit descends upon me; then a feeling of great warmth follows. At that moment, I am completely overpowered by the Holy Spirit, which gives me confidence and the complete assurance that all my movements come from the said spirit, which does the healing.

"As I place my hands on the patient's body, I feel the healing energy surge out through my fingers, causing vibrations and stimulating the cells of the patient's afflicted part. When in that state, I am not myself, or rather, there is another mind directing me. The said mind is so powerful it permeates my whole body and draws out the diseased tissues or waste matters that are causing pain and suffering. My hand at the moment is like a magnet that automatically attracts the diseased part.

"This healing energy or power within me, however, is not limitless. When it is consumed after a lot of healing, I return to my usual ordinary, humble self. I do not have a recollection of what I did in the healing session.

"When I open the body, there is no pain, for it is not my hand that does it, but the power that emanates from God. The human body is composed of cells that have tiny minds of their own and these cells receive instruction from either the instinctive or intellectual minds (which are still material) or from the spiritual mind.

"When my spiritual mind is attuned to the higher intelligence that is the Holy Spirit of God, my hands emit an energy that is more powerful than the physical constitution of the human cells, so that they merely give way to the more powerful force.

"However, in order for the healing to be truly effective, the patient must sincerely respond to the process. This is true for all forms of healing, whether orthodox or unorthodox. All healing is self-healing in the ultimate analysis.

"When the body is opened, there is a snapping sound, followed by a whizzing and splashing one. Only those who are spiritually attuned hear this strange sound, which is caused by the separation of cells as the body opens. Since the body is composed of almost 80 percent water, a splashing sound is heard as the fingers penetrate the body.

"All this, of course, sounds fantastic and unbelievable. But one hopes that someday scientists and doctors can explain the phenomenon in a more accurate way so that it can be taught in schools to relieve the suffering of mankind." (5)

Simple Energy Healing Techniques

Simple Energy Healing Techniques

◦━◈━◦

Sa kayano, anaa ang katahum.
In simplicity there is beauty.

Energy healing has been practiced around the world in different ways for thousands of years, and many books are available that outline how to use energy healing for your own well-being as well as that of others. This chapter gives simple instructions on how to use the tools I am the most familiar with—rather than repeating exercises described by other authors and healers. I use these methods on a regular basis in my own life and in my work as a magnetic healer.

There is much crossover of information, because all true healing paths are based on universal spiritual concepts. Of the many books that are available, these are my favorites: *The Power to Heal: a Concise and Comprehensive Guide to Energy Healing* by Robert Pellegrino-Estrich and the classic *The Psychic Healing Book* by Amy Wallace and Bill Henkin. Barbara Ann Brennan's *Hands of Light: a Guide to Healing Through the Human Energy Field* is also a useful resource, although it is quite detailed and requires extensive study. See the Additional Reading section for more information about these books. There are many workshops on how to do energy healing, and a search on the Internet or the listings in your local New Age or metaphysical magazine can help you locate the class that is right for you.

Every human being has the innate ability to heal and relieve pain. Healers do not have to be born clairvoyant nor have any special natural healing power. They only need to be sincere in their desire to help others. Here are some simple ways you can create more wellness in your life and in the lives of your friends and family:

1. Connecting to Divine Energy by Creating an Energy Cord to the Center of the Earth

Sit in a relaxed pose with your (shoeless) feet flat on the floor and your hands in your lap, palms up. Imagine (visualize) there is a cord attached to the base of your spine that goes down into the center of the earth. This cord can be any color or thickness that feels right to you, and it can be made of any material. Once you create your cord, it will always be available to ground you to the earth. All you have to do is think about it. Your cord can go through solid objects, even if you are on the top floor of a tall building or flying in an airplane, because it is made of energy.

Next, visualize a large ball of sparkling, golden light about a foot above your head—some people use a funnel or inverted pyramid instead of a ball. Slowly and gently, bring this light down in through the top of your head. See it moving throughout your body: your head, throat, heart, solar plexus, and abdomen. Send it down your arms and legs and back up to your abdomen. Finally, flush the light down through your grounding cord, taking with it any "dis-ease," illness, anxiety, anger, or other negative emotion or disturbance. This process is called *running energy*.

2. Connecting to Earth Energy Using Cords

Sit in a relaxed pose with your (shoeless) feet flat on the floor and your hands in your lap, palms up. Imagine there is a cord attached to the bottom of each foot that goes down into the center of the earth. Note that although many people talk about there being seven chakras—the areas of interconnection between the body and spirit—others believe there are more than seven, including chakras in the hands and feet.

Next, visualize energy from the center of the earth moving slowly and gently up towards you through these cords. Feel the energy enter your feet and begin to rise further up into your body until it has filled you completely. This energy is different from the Divine light brought in by the first exercise. It will feel thick and heavy, but not burdensome. This exercise is especially helpful when you are feeling anxious, fearful, overstimulated, hyperactive, or just generally "ungrounded." Try it the next time you are having trouble sleeping or you feel overly stressed.

These exercises can remove imbalances and energy blocks. They help create a new, more perfect pattern, or *blueprint*, which the physical body then begins to conform to, thereby improving health and bringing a greater sense of well-being.

3. Connecting to Divine Energy Using the Lord's Prayer

According to Edgar Cayce, the "Sleeping Prophet," recitation of the Lord's Prayer opens the chakras of the body, through which we are connected to Spirit. The seventh chakra, located at the top of the head, connects us to Universal Consciousness.

In his writings on meditation, Cayce discusses how each line of the Prayer is connected vibrationally to a specific endocrine gland, and how the recitation of the Prayer helps to cleanse and energize the glands and the entire body. The drawing on the next page, which is taken from Edgar Cayce's writings on meditation, illustrates the various glands, their corresponding lines of the Prayer, and their healthy vibrational colors. See edgarcayce.org for information about Edgar Cayce and his lifetime of dedication to the healing of humanity.

Begin your meditation on the Lord's Prayer by sitting in a relaxed pose with your (shoeless) feet flat on the floor and your hands in your lap, palms up. Breathe deeply and slowly say the Prayer silently to yourself, allowing the energy of the Prayer to fill you completely and bring you to a peaceful state.

I often do this meditation before going to bed. I also recite the prayer before I see someone for healing. Often I do not get past the second or third line because my seventh chakra opens and I receive what I call the "download." This is usually experienced as a massive wave of energy that fills my head, bringing with it information about the person I am about to meet for healing. Often, I also receive a "diagnosis" and a "treatment plan," which increase my knowledge about how I can best help the client.

When the person arrives and lies down on the table, I again recite the Prayer while lightly touching them, usually on the top of their head. If the client is Christian, or if the case is particularly difficult, as with cancer, I recite the Prayer out loud. Sometimes I ask the client

THE LORD'S PRAYER, THE ENDOCRINE SYSTEM, AND THE CHAKRAS (According to Edgar Cayce)

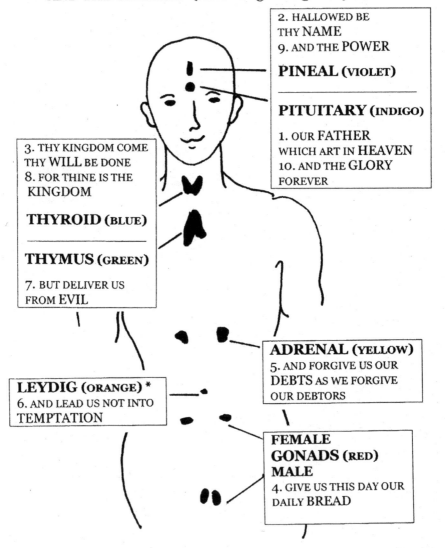

2. HALLOWED BE THY NAME
9. AND THE POWER

PINEAL (VIOLET)

PITUITARY (INDIGO)

1. OUR FATHER WHICH ART IN HEAVEN
10. AND THE GLORY FOREVER

3. THY KINGDOM COME THY WILL BE DONE
8. FOR THINE IS THE KINGDOM

THYROID (BLUE)

THYMUS (GREEN)

7. BUT DELIVER US FROM EVIL

ADRENAL (YELLOW)
5. AND FORGIVE US OUR DEBTS AS WE FORGIVE OUR DEBTORS

LEYDIG (ORANGE) *
6. AND LEAD US NOT INTO TEMPTATION

FEMALE GONADS (RED) MALE
4. GIVE US THIS DAY OUR DAILY BREAD

* LEYDIG (OR LYDEN)
The leydig gland is a small (pea-sized) gland in the urogenital system. Discovered in 1892 by anatomist Franz Leydig, this gland was regarded by Edgar Cayce to be the "seat of the soul" in the human body. In 1850, Franz Leydig also discovered the cells of leydig, which are now recognized as producers of testosterone in the gonads. Medical science has not yet discovered the leydig gland. From: www.edgarcayce.org.

to recite it with me. As I say the Prayer, healing energy pours into me through my seventh chakra and comes out through the palms of my hands and into the client. Sometimes, I also say silently to myself, "Let the Divine power of the Holy Spirit come unto me for the highest good of the person before me."

I believe that with sincere practice anyone can make a similar connection with the Divine by recitation of the Lord's Prayer.

4. Protection and Healing Using Spiritual, White Light

When dealing with stressful situations or troublesome people, you can protect yourself using this energy healing tool. Simply pull your mind back a bit from the situation and visualize your body encased in a tube of white, sparkling, spiritual light. Affirm that no negativity can pass through this protective light, although you will still be able to interact with those around you.

I sometimes use this tool when I am riding in a car with someone who wants to argue or who is otherwise excessively negative. In this case, I visualize a large sheet of white light between me and the person sitting next to me. Often this is all that is necessary to both protect myself energetically, *and* help the other person calm down. After all, it can be difficult to argue with someone who just smiles at you from behind an invisible, protective shield. Of course, you can remove the light when it is no longer necessary.

As discussed elsewhere in this book, I sometimes use this same white light during healing sessions by leaving a psychic bandage in place at the end of a session. I see this clairvoyantly as white light encircling an organ or area of the body that needs extra attention. In this way, the light continues to heal the client after they leave my presence. I believe anyone can do this by placing their hands, and their good intentions, on another as they visualize healing and nourishing Divine Light pouring through them and into the person they want to help.

5. Helping Friends and Family Using Energy Healing

Before doing any type of energy healing, perform the exercise described in number 1 above, in order to raise your own vibration as high as possible. After doing a healing, hold your hands and forearms under cold running water in order to release any negative energy you may have picked up. If running water is not available, you can visualize your hands and arms being bathed and cleansed with light.

The simplest method of healing is called "laying on of hands." (As discussed elsewhere in this book, this is called "magnetic healing" in the Philippines.) This is done by placing your hands on the afflicted part of another person's body and asking Spirit to heal them. This request is especially important to bring in Divine assistance. By placing your hands on another with love and the intention of helping them towards their highest good, you can transmit healing energy that will revitalize the person's etheric and physical bodies, remove blockages, create positive change at the molecular level, and improve the person's overall health and well-being.

6. Running Energy with Another Person

Ask the person you intend to help to lie on a massage table, or other suitable surface such as a bed or the floor. Sit at the person's head or feet and do the visualization described in number 1 above to fill yourself with Divine healing energy—or you can use the Lord's Prayer meditation described in number 3 above.

At some point during this process, you will become completely relaxed and full of light. When this happens, gently place your hands on the person's head (or feet) and visualize the healing light moving from your hands into them and filling their entire body, clearing out any disease or other negativity.

The tension and stress that often accompanies chronic pain sometimes intensifies the sensation of pain. This type of energy healing is especially helpful because it is soothing and can help relax people who are experiencing pain.

7. Aura Cleansing

As discussed throughout this book, in the Philippines, healing work is often done by a designated faith healer or psychic surgeon, but it is also done by others in the community. Usually in the evening, when the heat of the day has cooled, family and friends will gather at the bedside of someone who is ill. Forming a circle around the sickbed, hymns are sung while each person's hands are held facing outward towards the person lying on the bed. In this way, Divine love and energy are channeled into the sick person. Healing energy is also sometimes channeled in the same way into bottles of water. This water is then taken as God-given medicine.

After singing and channeling energy, the community members hold their hands 6 to 12 inches away from the sick person's body. Beginning at the head, they gently stroke the aura, or energy body, all the way down to the feet. This cleansing removes negativity from the energy field and offers comfort. Sometimes, when negative energy is encountered, you can see the healers removing "handfuls" of negative energy from the sick person, and throwing it away from the body and into the air. Barbara Brennan discusses a similar method of aura cleansing in her book *Hands of Light*.

This might be followed by laying on of hands by one or two people, if appropriate, but not the whole group at once because this much energy transfer would likely be too much for the ill person to absorb.

8. Aura Scanning

As you continue the practice of cleansing the aura, you will eventually be able to "scan" another person's energy body in order to identify specific problem areas. In my own work as a magnetic healer, I touch the client's head or feet lightly while saying the Lord's Prayer, until I become aware of dark energy in specific areas, signifying dis-ease. Sometimes I become aware of energy cords, as discussed earlier. From this, I know where to place my hands.

In order to become sensitive to the human aura, start by placing your hands about twelve inches from the person's head. Move your hands in slowly towards the body until you can feel a change in the energy emanating from them. Next, move your hands down the sides and front of the body (and back if the person is standing). Look for any changes in the shape or feel of the aura. If you are clairvoyant, watch for changes in color.

This exercise can be refined to focus on any of the main chakras in the body:

Seventh: Top of head (crown chakra)
> Color: white
> Endrocrine gland: pineal
> Related to higher mind
> Example of disturbance at this level: feelings of being cut off from God and personal experience of spirituality

Sixth: Forehead (the "third eye")
> Color: indigo
> Endrocrine gland: pituitary
> Related to celestial love
> Example of disturbance at this level: difficulty visualizing and understanding mental concepts; learning disabilities

Fifth: Throat
> Color: blue
> Endrocrine gland: thyroid
> Related to higher will
> Example of disturbance at this level: difficulty in assimilating information; confusion regarding sense of self; difficulty speaking personal truth

Fourth: Heart
> Color: green
> Endrocrine gland: thymus
> Related to love
> Example of disturbance at this level: difficulty trusting and loving others

Third: Solar plexus
> Color: yellow
> Endrocrine gland: pancreas
> Related to mental life

Example of disturbance at this level:
lack of self-esteem and confidence

Second: Genital area
Color: orange
Endrocrine gland: gonads
Related to the emotional aspects
Example of disturbance at this level:
inability to enjoy sexual relationships
and relate intimately with others

First: Base of the spine
Color: red
Endrocrine gland: adrenals
Related to physical function
Example of disturbance at this level: depression;
lack of will to live

Hold your hands over each chakra area for a few minutes—first in front of the body, then behind (if the person is standing). Look for different energy sensations and colors, especially dark colors. Pay attention to where you can feel energy leaving your hands or projecting from the person, or areas where there is no sensation, which indicate stagnation and/or illness. With practice, this exercise can lead you to an understanding of what parts of another person's body need loving attention.

Learning to heal energetically is like playing a musical instrument: the more you practice the more you will be able to do it.

"He called his twelve disciples to him and gave them authority to drive out evil spirits and to heal every disease and sickness."
Matthew 10:1

Epilogue

Epilogue

No sintaw a paggubbuatannu, sinay a paddannannu.
One ends where one began.

Joseph stands at the edge of the sugarcane field. He is still handsome, even though he is starting to lose his teeth. The wind begins to blow across Pangasinan, and he turns to catch the smell of the rain coming from the sea, far to the east. The rain will nourish the rows of tiny sugarcane seedlings he has just finished planting, but Joseph will not be here to reap this particular harvest, or those that follow. This work will fall to the tenant farmer who has rented Joseph's land.

It has been fourteen years since he loved the American girl. He knows now she is not coming back. She moves forward on the road between life and death, and soon he, too, will be leaving. Joseph has a visa for Spain, where he will join his wife and Mely's younger sisters, who are already working there. Joseph will become part of the great "Filipino Diaspora," like so many others.

Belen Ganagana, Mely's eldest sister, continues to live in Vacante. As of this writing, she is the head Bishop of the Faith in God Spiritual Church. Her husband has passed on, and her children are now bearing their own children, making Belen a grandmother many times over. She writes to me occasionally with news of the family, and to ask that I send more guitar strings because the humidity keeps rusting the ones they have. Belen's contact information can be found at the end of this book and anyone is welcome to visit.

Minchu grew up and graduated from high school. Luna married her "prince" and moved to the United States, although I do not think she realized her dream of becoming a lawyer, choosing instead to have a family. Trinidad went back to Bolinao after her mother died, and I have been unable to locate her. Ramon married the female security guard he hired to protect him from "bandits." The marriage only lasted a couple of years. The last I heard, he was traveling between Germany and India, and studying with a Hindu guru.

——✳——

Connie Arismende passed away in 2002. Although Marcos Orbito had given her many more productive years of life, she eventually died of kidney failure. The church in Lemmon Valley was sold and most of her family moved away.

——✳——

As for me, when I returned to California after psychic surgery with Jun and Yuko Labo, the doctor again told me I still had a small fibroid tumor. He was mystified as to why it had not grown larger. But, although it was small, and I no longer experienced severe pain and excessive bleeding, I did not follow my inner intuition and wait for the final results of the healings I had received. I acted out of fear instead of trusting the process. I was worried that my condition would get worse, and I might not have health insurance, so I decided to have medical surgery. In hindsight, I realize it was a hasty decision, and I wish I had waited for my physical body to catch up to my etheric healing.

I continue to receive miraculous benefits as a result of my time with the healers, and although Mely has left her body, she is a living presence I feel whenever I sit for meditation or give magnetic healing to others. She and the other healers taught me to live in the spirit. I came to them with my negativity, self-doubt, and narrow viewpoint, and left with a broader understanding of what it means to be both human and spirit. As I tune myself inwardly to meet Mely, I know that our true relationship lies in the silence between words. I experience her more now, after her death, than I did when she was alive. More importantly, I am no longer afraid of my own death, because I know where I am going when I leave my body—and I know who will be there to welcome me when I arrive.

Recently, Connie appeared in my meditation. She showed me a "picture" of her children and her husband, Coco. I understood that she had come to me only now because she had been busy taking care of her family from the other side. Mely also appeared. They were brilliant, golden light forms. They greeted each other as if Mely was also seeing Connie for the first time since they had both died.

A beam of light formed a triangle that went from the center of Mely's head to the center of mine, and then to the center of Connie's head and back to Mely. We were connected by the Holy Spirit, which appeared as the beam of light. Archangel Michael stood behind us. He was a glowing blue light, and his hands were raised above us in a blessing.

I felt the same way I had at the church in Vacante the first time the light flowed through the medium and into my hands and fore- head. As before, the light seemed to speak, directing me to let it flow throughout my entire body and into everyone I touch.

Although the physical presence of Filomena Naces is no more, she lives through me. We are the interplay of sun and shadow, the seen and the unseen. Through us moves the Holy Spirit, which blesses everything in the universe. Mely's final prophecy is complete—she speaks through my voice and hands. This is the *proof* that life does not end when the physical body dies. The spirit continues, and we can expect to meet each other again and again throughout eternity.

References: The Miracle and Enigma of Psychic Surgery

1. See: *www.healthwatcher.net* and *www.ncahf.org* for the skeptical viewpoint.

2. *PSI Healing* by Alfred Stelter; New York: Bantam Books, 1976.

3. See: *www.anubuddha.com*.

4. *Going Within: A Guide for Inner Transformation* by Shirley MacLaine; New York: Bantam Dell, 1989.

5. The quotes by Andreas Freund and Alex Orbito are from *The Magicians of God. The Amazing Stories of Philippine Faith Healers* by Jaime T. Licauco, National Bookstore, Inc., Manila, 1981. The quote by Alex Orbito (on page 179) also appeared in "Channel of Divine Healing" by Clifford Sawhney; *Life Positive*, February 2001.

6. *Faith Healing and Psychic Surgery in the Philippines* by Jesus B. Lava and Antonio S. Araneta; The Philippine Society for Psychical Research Foundation, 1982.

7. Quotes by Jaime Licauco are from an Internet article: "Faith Healing: Harnessing the Power Within" by Genevieve Ruth R. Villamin; *www.stii.dost.gov.ph/INFOSCIENCE/jun202/jun02_6.htm* (no longer accessible).

8. Adapted in part (with permission) from *Understanding Ilocano Values* by Tomas D. Andres; Giraffe Books, #7 Visayas Ave., 1128 Quezon City, Philippines, 2003.

9. *The First Voyage Around the World* by Antonio Pigafetta and Theodore J. Cachey; Marsilio Publishers, 1995.

10. See: *www.spiritwritings.com* and *www.sgny.org*.

11. *John of God: The Brazilian Healer Who's Touched the Lives of Millions* by Heather Cumming and Karen Leffler. Beyond Words Publishing: Hillsboro, Oregon, 2007.

12. *The Miracle Man: The Life Story of Joao de Deus* by Robert Pellegrino-Estrich; Australia: Triad Publishers Ply. Ltd., 1997.

13. *Kardec's Spiritism: A Home for Healing and Spiritual Evolution* by Emma Bragdon, Ph.D. Lightening Up Press: Woodstock, Vermont; 2004.

14. *www.crystalinks.com*.

15. Adapted in part (with permission) from *The Secret Teachings of the Espiritistas: A Hidden History of Spiritual Healing* by Harvey J. Martin, III; ISBN 0-966-08438-1. Metamind Publications, P.O. Box 5154, Canton, Georgia 30114-0266; *www.harveymartin.com*, 1998.

16. *www.nsac.org*.

17. "Spiritual Adventures" by John Huddleston; *www.psychic readernewspaper.com*.

18. *Psychic Surgery–A Guide to The Philippines Experience* by Donald A. McDowall; Cosmos Pty. Ltd., 1993. See also: *Healing: Doorway to the Spiritual World*; Cosmos Pty. Ltd., 1998; *The Truth About Sickness and Healing*; 1st Books, 2003; and *The Universal Intelligence of Spirits, Guides and God*; 1st Books, 2004.

19. *The Wonder Healers of the Philippines* by Harold Sherman; Los Angeles: DeVorss & Co., 1974.

20. *Teachings and Illustrations As They Emanate From the Spirit World* by Mary T. Longley. See also: *www.nsac.org* (National Spiritualist Association of Churches).

21. *Don't Kiss Them Good-bye* by Allison DuBois; New York: Fireside/Simon & Schuster, 2005.

22. *Arigo: the Surgeon of the Rusty Knife* by John G. Fuller; Devin-Adair, 1975.

23. *Mail Tribune*, Medford, OR; 1/26/07.

24. *How People Heal* by Diane Goldner; ISBN 1-57174-363-4; Charlottesville, NC: Hampton Roads Publishing Company, 1999.

25. *Wheels of Light: Chakras, Auras, and the Healing Energy of the Body* by Rosalyn Bruyere; New York: Fireside/Simon & Schuster, 1989.

26. See: *www.michaeltamura.com*.

27. *Why People Don't Heal and How They Can,* by Caroline Myss; Three Rivers Press: New York, New York, 1997.

Additional Reading

Some of the books listed in the Reference Section and below are out-of-print, but they can sometimes be found on *Amazon.com* and other Web sites.

Into The Strange Unknown by the Two Men who Lived Every Moment of It: Ron Ormond and Ormond McGill. Published in 1957 or 1959 by the Esoteric Foundation, California. This is the first known book in English on the subject of psychic surgery. It was written by two reporters who went to the Philippines. See *www.harveymartin.com* for Harvey Martin's commentary.

Faith Healers of the Philippines by Gert Chesi. 1981; Perlinger Publications. Generally unavailable, except in German.

The Path of the Dream Healer: My Journey Through the Miraculous World of Energy Healing by Adam; Plume/Penguin Group, 2006.

The Power to Heal: a Concise and Comprehensive Guide to Energy Healing by Robert Pellegrino-Estrich; ISBN 85-902898-2-6; Gráfica Terra, Goiânia, Brazil.

The Psychic Healing Book by Amy Wallace and Bill Henkin. North Atlantic Books: Berkeley, California, 2004.

Hands of Light: A Guide to Healing Through the Human Energy Field by Barbara Ann Brennan. Bantam Books: New York, New York, 1988.

People Who Don't Know They're Dead by Gary Leon Hill. Red Wheel/Weiser: Boston, Massachusetts 2005.

Healing and the Bible

Ang pananalig, ay landas ng tagumpay.
Faith is the way to Heaven.

Healing is discussed frequently in the Bible. People who believe in the laying on of hands, faith healing, and psychic surgery believe the miracles achieved by healers in modern times are the same as those of Jesus and his Disciples. Jesus often said that faith in God has the power to heal. The following are quotes from the Bible where healing is discussed.

Old Testament

Miriam is healed of leprosy.
Numbers 12:10–15

King Jeroboam receives a
   warning.
I Kings 13:4–6

The Lord appears to Solomon.
II Chronicles 7:14

My bones are weak.
Psalms 2:6

All His benefits.
Psalms 103:2–3

Delivery from destruction.
Psalm 107:20

He binds their wounds.
Psalm 147:3

To everything there is a season.
Ecclesiastes 3:3

A prophecy against Egypt.
Isaiah 19:22

We are healed by His suffering.
Isaiah 53:4–5

New Testament

The news of Jesus spreads.
Matthew 4:23–24

The man with leprosy.
Matthew 8:3–4

The faith of the Centurion.
Matthew 8:5–7

Jesus heals Mary.
Matthew 8:14–17

Jesus heals a paralytic and
teaches forgiveness.
Matthew 9:1–7

A dead girl is restored and a
sick woman healed.
Matthew 9:18–25

The blind men are healed.
Matthew 9:29

Jesus authorizes his disciples to
heal.
Matthew 10:1

Jesus instructs the twelve
disciples.
Matthew 10:5–10

Healing on the Sabbath.
Matthew 12:10–13

Healing at Gennesaret.
Matthew 14:35–36

Jesus heals the daughter of a
gentile.
Matthew 15:28

The woman who touched the
cloak of Jesus and was healed
by her faith.
Mark 5:25–29 and 34

A demon is driven out.
Mark 7:25–30

The healing of a deaf and mute
man.
Mark 7:32–35

Those who believe will be
saved.
Mark 16:16–18

Healing the broken-hearted.
Luke 4:18

Physician heal thyself.
Luke: 4:23

Thy sins are forgiven.
Luke 5:17–20

A maiden arises from the dead.
Luke 8:43–56

A crippled woman is set free
from infirmity.
Luke 13:10–13

Ten were healed of leprosy, but
   only one returned to give
   thanks.
Luke 17:11–19

A blind beggar is healed.
Luke 18:35–42

Jesus heals a nobleman's son.
John 4:46–53

The blind, the lame, and the
   paralyzed.
John 5:1–9

Jesus empowers others to do as
   he does.
John 14:12–14

By the temple gate called
   Beautiful.
Acts 3:2–10

Jesus instructs his disciples to
   heal in his name.
Acts 4:30

The sick and vexed with
   unclean spirits.
Acts 5:16

Aeneas is healed of palsy.
Acts 9:33–35

Paul heals the man from Lystra.
Acts 14:8–11

God heals through Paul.
Acts 19:11–2

The gift of healing by the one
   Spirit.
1 Corinthians 12:4–11

The power of faith.
James 5:13–16

The beast is healed.
Revelations 13:3

The river of life and the leaves
   of the healing tree.
Revelations 22:2–5

The gift of healing by the one
   Spirit.
1 Corinthians 12:4-11

The power of faith.
James 5:13-16

The river of life and the leaves
   of the healing tree.
Revelation 22:2-5

Finding a Healer

❧✦❧

The author and publisher of this book do not endorse any specific healer. If you are planning to visit the Philippines for the first time, consider going with a reputable tour guide—if you can afford the extra cost, which, in some cases, can be excessive. If you are an experienced traveler and are able to go on your own, call the healer you plan to visit before you buy your airplane ticket, in order to make sure the healer will be there when you are in the Philippines.

List of Healers: Thanks to the ongoing efforts of Godofredo "Butch" Stuart, M.D., a list of healers in the Philippines can be found at: *www.stuartxchange.com*. See also *www.aenet.org/philip/healers.htm*.

The Faith in God Spiritual Church: The church founded by Rev. Filomena Naces, is still active, and visitors are always welcome. Write to Rev. Avelina "Belen" Ganagana at: Faith in God Spiritual Church, Barangay Vacante, Binalonan, Pangasinan, Philippines 2436, or just show up for Sunday services (8 to 11 a.m.). To reach Vacante, take the air-conditioned Victory Liner bus from the Pasay Bus Terminal, just south of Ermita in Manila, north to Binalonon. (This is also the bus to Baguio.) Then hire a tricycle (rural version of taxi) to the church.

Rev. Ramon "Jun" L. Labo: The author spent three weeks with Jun Labo in March 2008 and had some very interesting experiences. Jun can be contacted by phone at: 0063-0917-885-9086, or write to him at: 444 Naguilan Rd., Baguio City, 2600 Philippines. Videos of Jun are available on the Internet at *www.YouTube.com*.

Rev. Alex Orbito: See: *www.pyramidofasia.org* for information about Alex Orbito.

John of God: Joâo Teixeira da Faria, also known as "John of God," has a healing center in Abadiânia, Brazil. See these Web sites for more information: *www.johnofgod.com*, *www.healingquests.com*, and *www.visitjohnofgod.com*.

Filipino Healing in Hawaii: Virgil J. Mayor Apostol practices the art of Ablon, a clinical form of manual medicine. He has also developed a unique approach to the spiritual science of bioelectromagnetic healing. See: *www.rumsua.com* for more information.

Travel Resources

∘⊶⊷✳⊶⊷∘

Accommodations

Many of the healers work in Baguio, so it might be best to consider flying there directly, thus avoiding the chaos of Manila. (The Baguio Airport is sometimes closed due to weather, so check ahead.) The climate in Baguio is moderate and more suited to people from cooler countries, and the hotels are well suited to foreign travelers. Healers located in Pangasinan Province can be easily reached by bus from Baguio.

However, if you do fly into Manila, the author recommends this safe, low-cost hotel, which has English-speaking staff and air-conditioned rooms:

Pension Natividad
1690 Del Pilar
Ermita District
Telephone: 63-2-521-0524

November–February are the best months to visit the Philippines, as the temperature is more moderate.

Air Travel

Flights to the Philippines can be expensive, but courier flights are a low-cost possibility for flexible travelers. Jupiter Air has courier flights from San Francisco and Los Angeles to Manila. See: *www.jupiter air.com* for information.

Filipino Publications (general topics)

Arkipelago Bookstore
The Bayanihan Community Center
1010 Mission St.
San Francisco, CA 94103

About the Author

Jessica Bryan is a professional book editor. In 2005, three of the books she edited for the American Academy of Neurology's patient series were nominated for the Foreword Award.

She is also the editor of several books published by Beyond Words Publishing of Portland, Oregon, including: *Cell-Level Healing* by Joyce Whiteley Hawkes; *JOHN OF GOD: The Brazilian Healer Who's Touched the Lives of Millions* by Heather Cumming; and *Animals in Spirit* by Penelope Smith.

One of the chapters in this book, "The Filipino Elvis Presley," has been accepted for inclusion in *Break Free, Break Rules, Break Bread,* a collection of travel stories and recipes edited by Rita Gelman, the acclaimed author of *Tales of a Female Nomad.*

The chapter entitled "The Wake" won the 2005 Writers Contest of the South Coast Writers Conference and was selected for publication in the Rogue River Echoes Anthology. "The Wake" and "The Filipino Elvis Presley" are on the Web at: *www.stuartxchange.org.* Jessica is also the author of *Love is Ageless: Stories About Alzheimer's Disease* (2002, Lompico Creek Press).

Jessica practices energy healing and does clairvoyant teachings in Talent, Oregon, where she lives with Tom Clunie D.C. and three Himalayan cats. Please feel free to e-mail: psychicsurgery@mind.net with questions or comments.

Permissions

The author personally thanks all of the great writers and teachers who have been quoted in this book for their wisdom, compassion, and inspiration. A thorough and extensive search has been conducted to determine whether previously published material included herein requires permission to reprint, or whether it is covered under Fair Use in the Copyright Act. If there has been an error, the author and publisher apologize, and a correction will be made in subsequent printings and editions. On this page, you will find the authors and publishers who have given permission to include excerpts of their published material.

Philippine Folk Literature: The Proverbs
Compiled and Edited by Damiana L. Eugenio © 2000
University of the Philippines Press
E. de los Santos St., U.P. Diliman
Quezon City, Philippines

Harvey J. Martin
Michael J. Tamura / *www.michaeltamura.com*
Hampton Roads Publishing / Diane Goldner
Mail Tribune / Scott Smith, Assistant Editor
Giraffe Books / Dr. Tomas Andres
Random House / Shirley MacLaine